Copyright © 2020 Steven Hromin
All rights reserved.

This text is dedicated to my family and to my wonderful girlfriend Rebecca. Thank you for supporting me and for making this endeavor possible.

Table of Contents

Introduction 1

Chapter 1: The Power of the Mind 4

Chapter 2: Budgeting 7

Chapter 3: Investing 22

Chapter 4: Student Loans 36

Chapter 5: Credit Card, Auto Loan, and Mortgage Debts 52

Chapter 6: Wedding and Marriage Planning 73

Chapter 7: Planning College for Your Children 79

Chapter 8: Planning for Retirement 92

Conclusion 114

Acknowledgements 116

References 118

Index 125

Introduction

Starting adult life on the right financial footing is desirable. I would argue that, for someone early on in life, taking steps to solidify your financial situation is probably the best decision you'll ever make. If you've started reading this book, you're probably wondering how you can gain knowledge into personal finance while simultaneously improving your financial situation. Your choice to read this book demonstrates your interest in improving your economic well-being. My goal in writing this book is to give you all the tools you need to help yourself succeed financially.

Before we delve into the topic at hand, I would like to offer my credentials to you. I want you to have confidence that the suggestions written here can help you succeed. I've been interested in personal finance since I was a teenager. Conversations with my parents about money and finance fueled my initial interest in the subject. I'm blessed to say that my parents were both financially secure and willing to share stories, anecdotes, and tips related to many relevant personal finance topics. These discussions further guided my interest and led me to ask many questions, further enhancing my knowledge of the subject. At the age of 17, I asked my father about stock investing and why it seems to be a popular topic of conversation. He gave me a book called *Stock Investing for Dummies*, the first of many I would eventually read concerning finance and investing. After reading the book cover-to-cover, I began researching stocks and subsequently made my first investment in 10 shares of Microsoft. I've also been investing since 2012, reading many books on the topic, and honing my skills and knowledge as it relates to personal finance subjects. Lastly, I'm a candidate within the Chartered Financial Analyst program, a set of three comprehensive exams designed to provide candidates with the tools and knowledge necessary to become a well-rounded financial professional in today's world. This is not to say that I don't have more to learn. However, I do want to provide color on my background because full disclosure allows my readers to judge for themselves whether I deserve credibility on the subject.

I chose to write this book because I believe that not enough people make financial matters a priority. Studies conducted by the Federal Reserve Board have shown that about one-third of Americans would struggle to procure $400 in an emergency. In a country so rich (in fact, #1 in GDP per capita for countries with over 10 million inhabitants), how we are so generally unable to keep our finances under control is simply startling. To the extent that the "consumer economy" has pressured Americans financially, I do not place much blame on the backs of American workers. Besides the struggle of attempting to keep up with the Joneses, Americans have to deal with the fact that real purchasing power hasn't increased materially since the 1970s (especially for the lowest income brackets). The COVID-19 pandemic is likely going to exacerbate this issue as many people have needed to use emergency cash withdrawals in light of job losses and other financial stressors. Finally, we don't emphasize financial literacy in high school coursework, so students need to rely on parents for vital insight on this topic. Unfortunately, because many parents did not learn about financial literacy in high school, they had to acquire much of their knowledge by trial and error. As it stands, parents have a tough time discussing money with their children. Some might not even know where to begin, while others might not have the initiative or believe it's a worthy cause.

As children, we often look to our parents for guidance. Sometimes, we develop the same habits they impart to us. Adapting this to personal finance, some individuals may have different experiences with money during childhood, and these experiences may manifest themselves as behaviors we exhibit in adulthood. I believe that being receptive to new information is the key to advancing yourself, regardless of your upbringing. As long as you're open to learning, I am confident that you can improve your financial situation.

The great thing about learning is that it never entirely

stops. There are things, financial and otherwise, that I'm learning every day, and it never ceases to amaze me how much information there is to consume. In picking up this book, your thirst for financial knowledge is apparent. Resolving to acquire knowledge is a monumental step towards the acquisition of knowledge itself. This point segues gracefully into the second key force, the lack of initiative to learn. Countless individuals are smart enough to handle ideas like compound interest, tax-efficient investing, and budgeting. However, they just don't set their minds to the task. Perhaps the stigma surrounding money doesn't help in this situation. As much as everyone seems to love having more money, seemingly few people want to discuss how to save, invest, and budget for the future. Getting back on topic, I do believe that a lack of initiative to learn about a given topic will make it very difficult to become proficient in that field. Your drive to acquire knowledge will help you connect the dots going forward.

    I am on a mission to provide you with the knowledge that will help you understand how to make your money best work for you. This endeavor will not translate to advice regarding specific investments. Instead, I shall encourage you to consider new ideas and courses of action which might not have crossed your mind before. Before we embark, I want to thank you for choosing to read this book. It has been a goal of mine to write a book for some time, and I'm grateful to be writing about something I love. Let's get started!

Chapter 1: The Power of the Mind

One of the keys to succeeding at anything you do is to have the right mindset. I consider it so important that I'm dedicating this first chapter to discussing how we think about money. As far back as I can remember, personal finance has been a fascination for me. I attribute this in large part to my upbringing. My parents have always strived to make financial matters a priority. This focus on finances heavily contributed to me making my first investment at the ripe, young age of 17. No matter your age, whether you're young or old, consider this: today is always a great day to get started. Dwelling on past mistakes is a recipe for keeping yourself stuck in your ways because feeling bad about yourself will lead to a self-fulfilling prophecy of negative habit formation. Be happy that you chose to educate yourself and start from there.

In discussing the mental fortitude and gameplan needed, I would like to divide this chapter into three sections. Here, I will lay out some of the more instrumental things to keep in mind as we move forward on this journey together.

Which Life Do You Want?

Attempting to make better financial decisions is an admirable undertaking, one that will require you to keep in mind your reasons for altering your mindset. Why are you choosing to shift from your previous state of mind to a new, retooled version of yourself? Perhaps you aspire to adequately prepare for retirement, build up an emergency fund to give yourself room to breathe, or save for a specific goal or event (such as a wedding or house purchase). The key takeaway here is that you should always be cognizant of your reasons for pursuing a habit change. Just by continuing to read this text, you have demonstrated that you are interested in furthering your financial potential. I am asking you to dig a bit deeper and to ask yourself, what are you looking to get out of this? What is the underlying impetus for the change in lifestyle you are seeking? Having these questions in mind will keep you focused on your ultimate financial goal, whatever that may be. When you recognize and understand the underlying reason for a change, you'll find a way to persevere through any adversity or doubt.

Living Within Your Means

The basic framework for building wealth starts with understanding one key point, which I will emphasize in bold: **to build wealth, you must live within your means.** There must be some excess capital beyond your spending that you can put to work for your future. A violation of this simple principle is the reason why we've seen individuals squander countless fortunes throughout history. Several examples include fortunes previously accumulated by the Vanderbilts, the Pulitzers, and the Hartfords. This same idea is why we sometimes see professional athletes broke after a few years of retirement, even after earning millions of dollars per year in the prime of their careers. If you resolve to keep this at the forefront of your mind when thinking about personal finance, you will have no issues putting the rest of this advice into action. You will be well on your way to financial security if you take note of this central idea.

Playing Both Offense and Defense

Much of the personal finance focus you'll find on the Internet will revolve around the expenses and savings side of the equation. There is no doubt that the principle of living within your means, combined with organically growing assets through investments, will set you up for future success. Having the self-awareness to cut costs and separate your needs from your desires is a great skill, and this is something we will touch upon later. However, these forums, blogs, and articles often forget to remind people of the benefits of increasing their income, and how this can aid in their goal to achieve financial freedom. Many of those who are currently struggling will find it easier to cut costs than to increase income. Still, I do think this point regarding income is worth making. I believe that investing time, money, and effort into your career will pay you substantial dividends in the future. It certainly helps if you like your chosen career as well, as you'll naturally be more inclined to pursue these extra-curricular opportunities. Unfortunately, the rewards for undertaking these actions can only be seen in hindsight, sometimes multiple years down the line. This delay is often why we don't see more people investing the "Big 3" (time, money, and effort) into their career growth. This book does not focus on guiding career growth. However, I would be remiss not to mention it as a potential catalyst for your success in achieving your goals. You can think of this idea in the context of a sports game, where your best-case scenario involves playing both great offense and great defense simultaneously. As much as the offense of your favorite football team wants to score a touchdown on every possession, you can be sure that the defense also wants to do their best to prevent the same from occurring within their endzone. To continue with this analogy, sometimes you will need to kick field goals, or be content with preventing a touchdown and allowing a field goal. If a different analogy works better for you, be sure to use it. The central point is that I would like you to think about your finances from both an offensive and defensive standpoint. The combination of these two strategies will aid in your quest to better your financial standing.

      With these ideas in mind, we can now move forward to the more technical aspect of personal finance. We will learn about the tools used and the methods employed to achieve our goals and lead us to the life we want, both today and in the future. I hope that you derive significant value from reading this book. Without further ado, let's get into it! In the next chapter, we will discuss budgeting and its use in achieving our goals.

Chapter 2: Budgeting

Before we begin to use our savings to invest or grow our net worth, we must first create a budget. Successful budgeting is at the heart of every financial operation, whether in the office or at home. Some people prefer to take a more reactive approach to monthly budgeting. This approach involves spending money before you've thought about where your money is going. In a sense, this can be described as "spend first, think about saving later." While this can work in the short-term, in the long run, it might lead to a lack of funds allocated to invest or save, which would bring us right back to where we started. If you put the work into this vital first step, you will be able to create a successful budget that will give you a great start to improving your financial well-being.

I want to emphasize that budgeting can often be the most difficult aspect of personal finance for many individuals. While it is perhaps the most important piece of the puzzle, most people don't want to talk about it. If you find it hard at first, that's okay. As with anything else in life, you will improve over time as you gain experience and comfort in this arena. Handling finances ultimately comes down to income minus expenses, so I cannot stress enough the importance of budgeting and staying diligent.

In starting to think about personal budgeting, it would be smart to quickly go over the most important financial statements used in business. This discussion will also come in handy later when we touch upon investments. All public companies in the U.S. are required to create three financial statements every quarter: the Income Statement, the Balance Sheet, and the Statement of Cash Flows. The Income Statement details earnings (i.e. profits) and expenses over a given period. The Balance Sheet serves as a snapshot of your assets and liabilities at a given point in time. These two documents are most useful for your purposes, so we will be sure to focus on them here. The income statement of a business serves as a useful template for your monthly budget. Using this framework, we can create our personal income statement, complete with all monthly incomes and expenses. Here, we will detail what goes in (income) versus what comes out (monthly expenses). Later on, we will also discuss how creating a personal balance sheet can help give you a clearer picture of your current assets and liabilities.

If you have a computer handy, open up a spreadsheet program, and create a new file for your first budget[1]. Microsoft Excel is a great tool to use for budgeting, as you can create multiple sheets within a file and keep track of everything in an organized fashion. For those interested in cloud-based software, I highly recommend Google Sheets. Excel comes preloaded with budget templates, which you can find by going to "File," then "New," then finally searching for the term "Budgets." The file titled "Personal Monthly Budget" contains several line items for relevant categories such as housing, entertainment, and transportation. This file also tallies projected line items and compares this to the value of your actual line items. Below is a screenshot of the sample monthly budget I created using this file (I've only inserted income for now, but we will get to discussing expenses shortly).

Sample Monthly Budget

Projected Monthly Income	
Income 1	$3,000
Extra Income	$300
Total Monthly Income	**$3,300**

Actual Monthly Income	
Income 1	$3,000
Extra Income	$300
Total Monthly Income	**$3,300**

Projected Balance (Projected income minus expenses)	$0
Actual Balance (Actual income minus expenses)	$0
Difference (Actual minus projected)	$0

We start by inserting our projected monthly net income. There are two income rows in case you earn money from a side job not related to your monthly salary. As you go through the months, you'll be able to see the trend between your projected and actual income and expense figures. From here, you can fine-tune your budget and increase its accuracy. Given that we only

---

[1] It is good practice to save the file before you begin your work, as doing so will prevent you from accidentally closing the file before saving.

need a few lines for income, this part of the process is generally pretty quick, and you'll often have a good sense of what your monthly net pay should be.

On the expense side, we see that this budget is granular in nature and comes with 58 line items. Feel free to ignore or delete any categories that you don't find relevant. We'll start by filling out the housing section because this category applies to everyone, and housing generally encompasses the most substantial monthly expenses of all groups. In this section, enter your projected costs for all relevant housing items, including mortgage or rent, phone, electricity, and gas. Next, hop over to the entertainment section and enter projected costs for movies, concerts, and any streaming services (which you can insert into one of the "Other" cells). Your mission, should you choose to accept it, is to fill out projections for all items that are relevant to you. Once you're ready, Cell J61 will show your total projected costs for the month. You can compare this to your total projected income in Cell C7 to see where you stand. If your projected budget doesn't balance, Cell H4 will show a non-zero number. If the number is negative, your projected expenses are higher than your projected income. To remedy this, you can look towards categories such as entertainment and personal care to see if you can reduce any of these expenses. These categories represent "wants" or items that you find desirable but not necessary for survival. Within the food section, dining out could be seen as a discretionary item, in case you need some slack. Cutting any items within the savings section should be regarded as a last resort only. We are looking to end our process with a Projected Balance of $0, meaning that the budget perfectly balances between income, expenses, and savings. I've included a screenshot on the next page that shows the housing and entertainment sections filled in.

HOUSING	Projected Cost	Actual Cost	Difference	ENTERTAINMENT	Projected Cost	Actual Cost	Difference
Gas	$80	$70	$10	Concerts	$100	$0	$100
Electricity	$50	$45	$5	Movies	$15	$10	$5
Mortgage or rent	$2,000	$2,000	$0	Netflix	$13	$13	$0
Phone	$50	$50	$0	CDs	$0	$0	$0
Water and sewer	$50	$50	$0	Sporting events	$0	$0	$0
Cable	$40	$40	$0	Live theater	$0	$0	$0
Waste removal	$0	$0	$0	Other	$0	$0	$0
Maintenance	$0	$0	$0	Other	$0	$0	$0
Supplies	$0	$0	$0	Other	$0	$0	$0
Other	$0	$0	$0	Other	$0	$0	$0
Subtotal			$15	Subtotal			$105

As of now, there is currently $120 unallocated because I didn't end up going to the concert, and movies, electricity, and gas cost less than I had projected. For the sake of simplicity, if we assume that I only spend money within these two categories, then increasing savings by $120 should balance this budget. Below is a screenshot of the change we can make within the savings section to offset the surplus of $120.

SAVINGS	Projected Amount	Actual Amount	Difference
Retirement	$0	$0	$0
Investment	$0	$0	$0
Other	$0	$120	-$120
Subtotal			-$120

If you look at the selected cell titled "Savings or Investments," you will see that we did not initially project any savings. Since we actually saved $120, inputting this into the "Actual Amount" column will result in a budget that is perfectly balanced on all sides. Take a look at the final screenshot on the next page for confirmation.

Sample Monthly Budget

Projected Monthly Income	
Income 1	$3,000
Extra Income	$300
Total Monthly Income	**$3,300**

Actual Monthly Income	
Income 1	$3,000
Extra Income	$300
Total Monthly Income	**$3,300**

Projected Balance (Projected income minus expenses)	$902
Actual Balance (Actual income minus expenses)	$902
Difference (Actual minus projected)	$0

By the end of the month, you'll be able to fill in all cells within the "Actual Cost" column. If you find that your Actual Balance from Cell H6 is non-zero, then you either have a surplus or a deficit within your actual activity for the month. If this figure is positive, you have excess over and above the actual costs you incurred, so this will be represented as extra savings (savings greater than what you intended to save during the period). If this figure is negative, then the sum of your expenses and savings would be greater than your income, so you are left with a negative balance. We are aiming for a balance of zero. If you happen to find that your balance is not zero, you will need to investigate and see why this is the case. For positive balances, this could simply mean that we intended to save $200 into a checking account but we actually saved $300, creating a $100 balance. Once we find where the difference lies, we will adjust the line items accordingly and ultimately end up with an Actual Balance of $0. This method of budgeting is called "Zero-Based Budgeting." It is popular because it instills the idea that every dollar has a purpose and that proper allocation can help us achieve our financial goals.

Now that we've discussed how to use an Excel template to create a budget, I would like to show you how to create a pen-and-paper budget that I like to use myself. You can also use this method on the computer, but here I've described it using paper in case some of you would like to go old-school. This budget involves many of the concepts that we just went over, though it is not zero-based. Your final balance will indicate the amount you will be able to save, assuming your projected income and expenses come to fruition. We will primarily use two columns, one for line item names and another for the dollar amounts. We can start by listing our primary source of income towards the top of the sheet. Within the amounts column, let's write our expected take-home pay for the month for which we are planning. Once we complete this step, we can skip one row on our sheet and begin to list our expenses for the month. I like to start by listing the largest expenses first, so mortgage/rent, groceries, and other essentials will comprise the top portion.

I also think it's important to divide all of your monthly expenses into one of two categories: needs and wants. Your needs will encompass the line items you need to survive and sustain your current standard of living. The three items mentioned above, as well as heating/AC, insurance, and water are all examples of things we all need in today's world. Another key need for many people is the payment on a student loan. This expense is often the second largest in size after rent or a mortgage. Any debt payments, including those for credit cards, should be included within needs as well.

Conversely, your wants will encompass the line items you would ideally like to possess but are more discretionary in nature. Internet, cell phone plans, cable television, and miscellaneous discretionary spending for leisure time are all examples of items we could consider our wants. By the nature of the categories, our wants are more likely to vary than are our needs because we all have different personalities, interests, and hobbies. I recommend that you highlight needs and wants separately, so you can easily keep track of these two categories. While undertaking this process is not easy, you are bettering your financial future by doing so. Great job!

In going through your list, you might find that some items could belong to both groups. Some might regard internet access, smartphones, or computers as crucial for both their entertainment value as well as their utility in keeping ourselves competitive within the workplace. I certainly won't argue that internet access is strictly a need or a want. For my budget, I like to label these items under "wants," but you will need to make this determination for yourself. As long as you match each item to one category, you will be able to analyze your spending. From this, you can draw conclusions that can help guide you in the future.

After we list our relevant income and expenses for the month, we are then able to sum up the expenses and compare this figure to our income. Go ahead and take income, subtract expenses, and take a look at the resulting total. If your result is a positive number, congratulations! Your current projection indicates that you will save money this month. However, if you see a negative number, please do not fret. This situation is common, and we'll work together to make sure you give yourself the best possible chance to save money.

To help give you a good sense of what financial experts typically recommend, I would like to take some time to discuss a popular method of budgeting: the "50/30/20" rule. This rule-of-thumb strategy involves allocating 50% of your pay to needs, 30% to wants, and 20% to savings (which is the income minus expenses number we calculated before). For example, a budget with a net pay of $2,000 would result in $1,000 for needs, $600 for wants, and $400 for savings. Depending on your situation, you might have a tougher time achieving this without making a concerted effort. You will likely need to allocate more than 50% of your pay to fund necessities in areas such as New York City, Chicago, and Los Angeles. This method of budgeting, like many others, offers a handy starting point. The details, however, will be left for you to fine-tune. Ideally, we would like to spend no more than 80 to 85% of our take-home pay on total expenses, which would leave 15 to 20% for savings. This built-in buffer will give us options: we can save the money directly as cash, invest the money for future growth, or pay down debt at a faster clip. I will be further discussing how we can edit our budget to give us a bit more wiggle room. This endeavor will allow us to increase our buffer and put more money to work every period.

When we look at our budget, we might initially regard many of the items as those that are necessary. Things such as rent and utilities will be sticky because they are often fixed or designed to operate within a tight range. Similarly, grocery costs are consistent over time because we all need food to survive.

Conversely, some might find that reducing coffee runs from two times a week to one time a week is a more manageable endeavor. We absolutely must take your current financial situation into account when making these decisions. However, as much as finances are essential, we also must consider your personal situation as well. Are you willing to make drastic changes? Are you more inclined to start small, perhaps starting with smaller budget items and slowly progressing to larger items once you feel comfortable doing so? Depending on how different your current buffer is from the optimal level, you might not need to make drastic changes at all. I think the best way to find out what works best for you is to try different things, get a sense of how you react, and adjust accordingly. I can tell you from experience that cutting spending on items we love is no easy task.

Finding more affordable ways to suit our needs isn't a walk in the park either. If I were looking for things to cut, I would probably look first at impromptu coffee runs, take-out, and any memberships that go unused every month. Keep in mind that these suggestions don't imply that you should cease these activities altogether. Instead, you can look into your line item figures and see whether you can realistically reduce any of them and still be happy. For me, I know I'm indifferent to buying coffee out versus making it at home. Don't get me wrong; I love a good latte or frap from Starbucks! However, I don't have a line item in my budget for coffee because it's not a regular activity for me. I drink more coffee at home than I do out of the house, so this would be factored into groceries and not treated as a separate category. On the other hand, someone who places a higher value in grabbing coffee or other treats before work might want to keep this as a separate item.

You might be wondering how we should account for hobbies within our budget. One of my biggest hobbies is collecting vinyl records, so I allocate a small portion of my monthly budget to pursuing this interest. I recommend that you try to do the same with your hobbies. It might be beneficial to do this for several reasons. First, you'll be able to see your hobbies and their related expenditures on paper. This action could lead to better organization of your thoughts. For myself, I know it helps to be more granular when listing my entertainment items. Also, you'll be able to allocate funds to a specific purpose, one in which you are deeply interested and excited to pursue. This allocation might sound restrictive, but it's a very liberating feeling. During the month, you'll have the freedom to spend your allocated amount on your hobby without feeling guilty about your spending. There is certainly a point you can reach where you are so specific about every line item that you start to lose the bigger picture; we don't want that to happen here. For example, I have a line item in my budget for miscellaneous weekend expenses. This line encompasses trips to the local restaurant, dates with my significant other, and unexpected outings to the store where urgency is necessary. For myself, I don't see the need to write down every trip to the store as a separate line item because we are primarily interested in our monthly spending. The level of detail that will work best for you is an aspect of budgeting that will depend heavily on your personality. I implore you to tailor your strategy to fit your preferences, while also making sure that the end product helps inform you about yourself. Your objective is to take steps that will bring you closer to accomplishing your goals, and fine-tuning your strategy will help in this manner.

So far, we've discussed the defensive aspect inherent within budgeting. I would now like to touch upon how we can play offense with our finances. If you are a salaried worker, you are most likely unable to increase your income until you have your next performance review. You might be on a yearly schedule, or you might have another arrangement depending on your specific job. As I mentioned previously, I do think it's worth your time to think about whether you are interested in career progression as your primary driver of income growth. If so, many fields have exams to take and certifications to earn, which can increase your standing and allow you to command higher pay. However, this will depend on the career you've chosen. I think this could be a better use of time, effort, and money than performing side jobs assuming your field has opportunities available. If you'd prefer to explore other avenues, there are a few options here.

One idea is to look for weekend opportunities to wait

tables, which can bring in significant tip income during certain times of the year. Another approach is to use some of your free time to drive for a ride-share service (provided you own a car). A final suggestion is to do mini-projects on websites. Some sites act as a marketplace for buyers and sellers of things such as completed art projects, Excel spreadsheets, and many other services. Aside from advancement within your primary career, these activities represent opportunities to supplement your main source of income. With a little effort on both the offensive and defensive side of your budget, it has a two-pronged effect on your savings buffer. For example, if you currently calculate a monthly buffer of $400, cutting an expense of $100 and earning another $100 during the month increases your buffer to $600. As mentioned, most personal finance material focuses on the expense side of the equation, so I do think there is value to be added in thinking this way. Whether you live in a busy city or a more relaxed rural setting, there seem to be ample opportunities for those who are willing to search out and seize them.

Throughout this chapter, we've talked about why we want to budget, how we want to set up our system, and how we can help ourselves on both offense and defense. Now, I want to discuss how we can use the buffer to our advantage. In sum, there are three uses for our buffer: increase our cash levels, pay down debt at a faster rate, or invest in growing our funds. I believe that creating an emergency fund is one of the fundamental keys to managing your finances. To this end, I will start by discussing how we can use our buffer to increase cash levels before we move onto extra debt repayments.

It might be prudent to define an emergency fund and its relevant uses. An emergency fund is an account where money is saved and kept but only spent during an emergency which necessitates expenditures exceeding those already in your budget. Simply put, it's money that is there when you need it the most. Most people, when they're starting adult life, aren't quite sure how much they should have in the bank. Is $1,000 enough? Perhaps $2,000 suffices? To answer the question, I believe that the often-recommended three to six months of living expenses is a great goal for us to set. Calculating the proper range for us shouldn't be too difficult. In fact, from our earlier chat about budgeting needs and wants, we have a solid idea as to the extent of our monthly necessities. We can take our total monthly needs and multiply it by 3 to get our lower bound and take our total monthly needs and multiply it by 6 to get our upper bound figure. By way of example, if our total monthly needs are $2,000, then our recommended emergency fund would range from $6,000 on the low end to $12,000 on the high end. If you're not able to put any current funds towards building your fund, you can still get there within one year if you allocate a buffer of $500 per month. Similarly, if we start with $1,200, we reduce our allocation from $500 per month to $400 per month.

As mentioned, I wouldn't worry if you're not yet in a position to allocate current funds to your emergency fund. Still, I do think it's incredibly important to think about how we can use our monthly surplus to build a safety net. If unexpected circumstances arise, it's much better to be prepared and to have easily accessible funds, ready to be used when needed. Unfortunately, these situations happen more often than you might think. Think about a car breaking down, and how expensive it can be to fix whatever prevents the car from operating normally.

Similarly, unexpected medical expenses or a prolonged period of unemployment can happen to anyone. If it happens to you, you'll be grateful to have financial peace of mind. It's essential to understand that the primary utility derived from this initiative is the peace of mind and freedom that comes with being prepared for an emergency. Once you've achieved this, you'll find yourself feeling much more free and able to take risks with allocating your capital. We will further lean into risk-taking after a discussion on tackling our debts, which will further help free up money and continue us on the path to wealth creation.

Once you are satisfied with your emergency fund, I think it's a great idea to take a look at the liabilities side of your financial picture. If you currently have any loans or debts outstanding, I encourage you to compile all the relevant documents together. It's a good idea to have everything in front of you while you're making important decisions. If it's helpful for you, feel free to type into your budget sheet the total amount outstanding of the loan and the applicable interest rate you are paying. This information should be available within your loan documents. You can also include your minimum monthly payment here as well. Two debt repayment strategies are very popular with readers, namely the debt avalanche method and the debt snowball method. The debt avalanche method involves making minimum payments on all debts and then using the extra funds to pay off the highest interest rate debt as quickly as possible. Mathematically, this approach will save you the most money in the long run, so it is vital to know of this as you go forward within your journey.

However, as much as personal finance involves math and numbers, we cannot ignore the emotional side also at play. Enter the debt snowball method. This strategy involves making minimum payments on all debts. However, instead of allocating extra funds to the highest interest loans, we would allocate these funds to obligations with the smallest outstanding balances. Dave Ramsey, one of America's most popular personal finance gurus, is a big proponent of this method. He frequently cites the positive psychological effects it has on its users as a reason for his support. I prefer the avalanche method for myself, but I do believe it's good practice to highlight multiple options for paying down debt.

To illustrate an example of both methods: say you have three loans outstanding, one for $10,000 at 5%, another for $20,000 at 7%, and one for $5,000 at 3%. Under the avalanche method (the first method discussed), we would allocate all funds available above the minimum payments towards the $20,000, 7% loan. The $20,000 loan has the highest interest rate that we are paying, so we will allocate funds here. Conversely, under the snowball method, we would allocate all funds available above the minimum payments towards the $5,000, 3% loan. The $5,000 loan has the lowest balance remaining, so we will try to knock it out first and unlock a substantial psychological boost.

If you have any outstanding debts, you most likely have a line item for each obligation you have. These line items can serve as your minimum payment for now, or you can choose to pay above the minimum for any loans, provided you have the buffer to support this choice. Now that we've learned about two of the most popular debt repayment strategies, we can use this knowledge to put these strategies into practice. If you're someone who might have a bit more internal motivation, using the debt avalanche method should help you save money on interest over time. Conversely, if you'd prefer the psychological benefit of seeing your loans being knocked out in succession, using the debt snowball method should be a better fit for you.

 I do want to say that I commend all of you who are looking to better your financial future by tackling your debt. The debt situation in America has worsened in three major areas: mortgages, credit cards, and especially student loans. A sizable number of people reading this right now may have student loans outstanding. This situation has made it more difficult for younger adults to purchase homes, save for their own children's college costs, and save for their retirement as well. It's going to take substantial work to fix this situation. Even so, I'm confident that, with hard work and the right mindset, you will achieve your goal of financial freedom. I hope the advice in this text speaks to you and gives you the strength and confidence you need to help yourself. You can do this!

 So far, we've talked about two of our buffer allocation options: increasing our cash levels through the creation of an emergency fund and paying down faster debt to save on interest over time. To round out the conversation on best buffer allocation, I will talk about how investing can help accelerate the growth of our assets (and, by association, our net worth).

 In thinking about investing, I would be remiss not to mention the wonderful powers of compound interest. It can help us achieve goals we might not have thought possible. There are two types of interest: simple interest and compound interest. For simple interest, you receive a percentage on the amount of your initial principal, without compounding. As an example, let's say you loan $1,000 to a friend at 5% simple interest, paid over two years. Under this scenario, payment to you will total $50 in the first year (interest only), and $1,050 in the second year ($50 in interest and your initial principal of $1,000). To clarify, you essentially bought a bond from your friend. This bond pays simple interest and does not allow for compounding. As such, all payments except the final one are based on the same amount of principal. To demonstrate, we can extend this idea out to 5 years. In this case, we would earn $50 in interest in Years 1 through 4, and then receive the final payment in Year 5 of $1,050. Our return on investment here would be 5%. This example is a good representation of how simple interest works. You start with a principal amount and receive payments based on the initial principal, but with no opportunity for increased payments due to compounding. However, with compound interest, money grows onto itself over time. Let's say that we start with an initial principal of $1,000, and our investment appreciates by 5% every year. After the first year, our investment would be worth a total of $1,050 ($1,000 of initial principal and $50 of interest). After the second year, our investment would add 5% to the Year 1 balance of $1,050, and our Year 2 balance would be $1,102.50 (a 5% gain on the Year 1 balance of $1,050).

A common framework to take advantage of compound interest is through investing in stocks, which gain or lose value depending on expectations regarding the economy, business results, and many other factors. We can also see compound interest within savings accounts. As the months go by, interest accrues monthly on the account balance. This process applies to both the initial principal as well as any added funds during the given periods. Most traditional banks offer lower interest rates than do their online counterparts. The difference is quite stark, with most banks paying approximately 0.09% per year, while high-yield savings accounts from online banks such as Ally paying about 0.60% per year. Of course, this difference won't make anyone rich on its own. I do think it's important to consider the effects of this spread over time due to compound interest. For a $10,000 deposit and a time horizon of 20 years, an interest rate of 0.09% leads to a final balance of $10,181.55. In contrast, an interest rate of 0.60% leads to a final balance of $11,270.93. This example shows the power of compound interest as a wealth-building mechanism if we use it wisely.

We've gone over several strategies and pointers to help you budget your money more effectively. However, more than anything, you'll need accountability if you want to achieve success. It's easy enough to talk about setting up a budget or tracking expenses. However, many people become discouraged and fall off the wagon after a few months of trying to keep a budget. We've all been in this situation. What will matter more than your ability to penny-pinch will be your diligence to continue on this journey, recognize mistakes, and improve your system.

Within this second chapter, we discussed the following:

- We looked at several key points regarding setting up a budget, including budgeting techniques such as using spreadsheet software and keeping track of all relevant categories. We also looked at Zero-Based Budgeting as well as a more traditional model of comparing income to expenses and examining the buffer through this lens.
- We talked about why we go through the trouble of creating a budget in the first place. We aim to accomplish several things here, including tracking our spending, analyzing our line items, and projecting our needs into the near future.
- We also saw how to pay ourselves first using budgets and proper allocation of expenses.

I am very confident that, armed with both the guidance provided here as well as your ambition and drive to succeed, you will set yourself on a path to great prosperity. I'd like to dedicate the next chapter to investing, which was discussed briefly in the preceding two paragraphs. We cannot properly examine this topic within only two sections, and its importance to our success cannot be understated.

Chapter 3: Investing

It's possible that, for some of you, investing has mostly been out of sight and out of mind. You might have heard family or friends discussing investing and markets, but never really understood its purpose. Perhaps you wanted to learn more, but you didn't know where to start. Unfortunately, all of these feelings and situations are very common. People are often unsure of how to start because there is so much information out there that it becomes overwhelming.

Similarly, others are afraid of losing their hard-earned money. Some have debts that are mounting against them, which makes it difficult to start putting excess capital to work. All of these reservations are completely reasonable. My goal is that, after reading this chapter, you will leave with a solid understanding of the different investment options available to you, as well as the implementation of these options within an investment strategy. Since stocks represent the best profile in terms of accessibility and functionality, we will focus on stocks in this chapter.

The stock market is a collection of publicly-traded companies. For each of these companies, a stock exchange lists the company under a specific symbol, called a ticker. Stock exchanges represent designated areas where stocks (and other investment vehicles) are traded. Exchanges are open for trading on most business days of the year, but occasionally have a recess for certain holidays. Some of the most prominent stock exchanges in the United States include the New York Stock Exchange, the NASDAQ, and the American Stock Exchange. Stocks are organized within different indices, which attempt to track the performance of a basket of companies. The type of companies that are tracked by a given index depends on the objective of the index itself. For example, the Dow Jones Industrial Average, perhaps the most well-known index in the world, tracks the performance of 30 large U.S.-based corporations. The other two most popular stock indices in the U.S. are the S&P 500 and the NASDAQ Composite. The former is made up of the 500 largest U.S-based publicly-traded companies, and the latter is made up of more than 3,300 common stocks, which can be based in countries all over the world. To clarify the last point, NASDAQ Composite has a heavy focus on American companies, specifically American tech companies.

Stocks can be separated into different classifications based on their size, which is measured by a metric called market capitalization. This simple calculation involves multiplying the number of shares outstanding by the price of one share. There are several categories that differentiate between companies based on market cap. The categories are as follows:

- Large-Cap (market caps greater than $10 billion).
- Mid-Cap (market caps of between $2 billion and $10 billion).
- Small-Cap (market caps less than $2 billion).

For simplicity's sake, we can categorize two of the three indices mentioned above in the following ways: the S&P 500 serves as a benchmark for Large-Cap stocks, and the Dow Jones Industrial Average serves as a benchmark for blue-chips, which is a common nickname for the largest companies within the Large-Cap category. The NASDAQ Composite is noticeably absent from this categorization because it doesn't have a focus on market cap, but instead has several listing requirements that must be met before a company joins the index.

To set ourselves up for successful stock investing, we should be sure to understand how our investment fits into the framework of a company. There are several different options that companies have to raise capital: they can issue common stock, preferred stock, or various debt maturities. We don't need to worry much about preferred stock or debt, but I do want to explain common stocks here as this is what people mean when they talk about the stock market. Common stocks represent a claim on the assets and future earnings of the firm. Stocks, also known as equities, do not have an expiration date. They derive their value ultimately from the value of the existing assets of the business, as well as all future cash flows into perpetuity. In contrast, bonds often pay investors a fixed rate per period and do not allow for residual profit payouts. Residual profits include any money that is left after a company pays all expenses for a period and makes all necessary investments to keep the business running successfully. Additionally, debt gets paid first both during a company's life and during bankruptcy. For these reasons, the risk is higher in equity than in debt because there is no guarantee that profits will eventually flow down to the shareholders. Because of this added risk, investors demand higher returns from stocks than from bonds, and the historical data shows that stocks have outperformed bonds over long periods.

As mentioned, the world of stocks is vast. However, it only has to be as complicated as you make it. You can choose to only research companies with which you are already familiar. Peter Lynch, one of the best investors in recent history, has avidly supported the strategy of buying what you know. He argues that individual investors have an advantage here because bureaucratic rules or short-term performance pressures do not constrain them. Therefore, they can take more risks and stick with stocks longer than can institutional investors. For you folks reading this on your Kindle, Amazon might be an excellent example of a company that offers a product that you use and enjoy.

Similarly, most Americans seem to be very familiar with the biggest tech companies in the world (Amazon, Apple, Facebook, Google, Microsoft, and Netflix). If you want to expand your knowledge of other companies or industries, you can learn a lot in the process. The strategy popularized by Peter Lynch relates to a concept developed by Warren Buffett and Charlie Munger from Berkshire Hathaway: staying within your circle of competence. Your circle of competence includes all ideas and businesses that you fully understand and readily grasp without much issue. If you're someone who loves buying cosmetics, your circle of competence would include companies that operate in the beauty space (such as Ulta, Sally Beauty, and Coty). For newcomers, I think staying within our circle of competence is a great strategy and reduces the likelihood that we'll overextend our capabilities. I encourage you to write down several companies with which you are very familiar, as well as why you enjoy purchasing goods or services from those companies. You'll become familiar with researching companies, which will become crucial as you become a better-educated investor. You'll also begin to recognize how you can use your current knowledge base to get a better feel for markets and investing.

Stock prices generally increase over time because corporate earnings increase as workers become more productive and as better technology allows for the efficient facilitation of business. Population growth will also contribute to growth in both GDP and earnings. Investors track many different macroeconomic indicators that give color to the state of the economy at large. These are important to understand, but for our purposes, I think it's best to build an understanding of microeconomic factors and what it means to be a shareholder before discussing macro statistics. Plainly stated, being a shareholder of a company means that you are entitled to any future residual profits earned by the firm during the period for which you own the shares. If I buy 1 share of Facebook stock (ticker: FB), I have a claim to the residual profits earned by Facebook attributable to my 1 share. Dividends represent an important avenue through which companies send payments to shareholders. These payments are often made quarterly. However, not all companies pay dividends at all points in time. Younger companies with better growth prospects tend to delay paying dividends because they see opportunities to deploy capital elsewhere and earn higher returns for shareholders. If they are successful here, then the stock price should increase over time as investors recognize the enhanced profit potential due to previous management decisions.

Repurchasing shares represents another method of payment to shareholders. This endeavor reduces the number of shares outstanding. This action increases the earnings per share (EPS) figure by distributing the same amount of profits to fewer shares after a repurchase. Shares outstanding represent small pieces of company ownership. For example, if a company has 100 shares outstanding and I own 1 share, then I would own 1% of the company due to my ownership of 1% of the shares. Public companies have much higher quantities of outstanding shares, generally at least 50 million shares and sometimes as many as 8 billion shares. The Board of Directors of a company authorizes buybacks and issuances. Just as buying back shares will increase profits per share, issuing new shares will decrease profits per share (because shares outstanding will increase). Repurchasing shares and paying dividends are the two avenues through which a company can return capital to shareholders.

Stocks are generally priced at a multiple of its current or future earnings. This multiple is called the "Price to Earnings Multiple," also known as the "P/E Multiple" or "P/E." It will be important to specify the type of earnings per share we use. Here, we can say "trailing twelve months" to mean the earnings per share for the most recent twelve months of business operation. As an example, we can imagine a stock priced at $100 per share, which has trailing twelve months ("TTM") earnings per share of $10. In this case, the stock has a P/E multiple of 10x.

When a company has negative earnings, the market generally uses a Price to Sales multiple to value stocks (since sales cannot be negative). This situation is commonly seen when a company is young and is more focused on growing revenues than it is on generating current bottom-line earnings. Recognizing the importance of earnings and sales multiples will allow us to evaluate fruitful opportunities in the future. Sometimes, you'll notice people proclaim that a company's stock is expensive because it has a high price per share. This heuristic might not be the best way to evaluate stocks because two companies can have different earnings per share. It can get confusing because some people think of it as buying a product in the store, where one bottle of cleaning spray shouldn't cost too much more than the next bottle. However, a share of Facebook and a share of Amazon are not very comparable on a price per share basis because Amazon has earnings of around $20 per share, whereas Facebook currently earns about $6 per share on a TTM basis. Similarly, sometimes I notice people saying that a stock is expensive because it has rallied significantly from its previous levels of a few weeks ago. The stock could be expensive on this basis, but it depends on how the business performs going forward and whether the current valuation is justified by the future potential of the company.

If you're looking to get started with learning about how financial markets work, I would recommend immersing yourself into the language of the business world. If you have cable, you can turn on CNBC or Bloomberg Television and try to adapt some of the vernacular used. Listening to news can help give you a good sense of what's happening within the world of business. You'll learn about company earnings, critical macroeconomic indicators, and develop insights into the current market sentiment. You can also start reading financial news online to supplement your knowledge base. Sites like CNBC and CNN have free financial news articles written without much jargon, which will help you relate the stories to yourself without feeling overwhelmed. I would stick to free resources as I wouldn't want you to purchase paid news access before you try the free options available to you. I can speak for CNBC as the articles aren't too long, are written in plain English, and often have critical points highlighted at the top of the webpage. Financial news websites will usually cover topics spanning across several asset classes, including stocks, bonds, commodities, and currencies.

One of the most crucial points to understand about stock investing is that having a long-term focus gives you the best chance for success. In the short-run, stocks can be very volatile and don't always correctly reflect business values. In fact, at any given point in time, a stock's market price can differ materially from a fair price derived by a rational investor. As such, it's best to consider both your time horizon and your risk tolerance when deciding how to invest. Funds needed within the next five years might not have a place in the stock market. The volatility in the short-term increases your risk of withdrawing funds at a less-than-favorable valuation level. A timeline longer than five years will allow you to ride out any waves that occur on either a macro or micro-level. Whether the entire market suffers a downdraft or one of your companies underperforms, this timeline should help smooth out volatility. In reading books from some of the greatest investors in recent memory, I've done my best to adopt a long-term focus on underlying business performance. To this end, it is important to recognize that as a shareholder of a company, you are a minority owner of the business and are self-interested in seeing the company succeed in the future.

In "The Intelligent Investor[2]," Benjamin Graham illustrated the above idea by stating that a market is a tool for investors to use when it is convenient for them. If you're looking to buy a house as a primary residence, you wouldn't be checking the market price constantly. You would only be interested in evaluating market prices when you're interested in selling and moving to a new residence for a better opportunity. This principle can be applied to stock investing, where we evaluate the business (not the stock) and expect to own the business for some time. When we buy shares of a company, we are wagering that, within a reasonable time frame, the rest of the market will see the same picture of the company that we see.

A relevant idea is the notion of the Efficient Market Hypothesis. This theory states that markets are efficient at all points in time and accurately reflect all known information about the company and the overall economy. I've found that market participants often try their best to consider new information when evaluating stocks (this is often called "pricing" information into stocks). However, this doesn't mean that the market can't be wrong on a particular stock. I'm blessed to say that I've taken advantage of several opportunities in the market that have worked out very well. You can do this as well, especially if you continue to do three things:

1) Stay within your circle of competence.
2) Expand your circle of competence to gain access to more opportunities.
3) Think of buying stocks as buying underlying businesses (becoming a part-owner).

---

[2] I highly recommend "The Intelligent Investor." It is a text that will dive into how Ben Graham thinks of investment opportunities and how you can better your mindset regarding investing. The book also details some of the most common pitfalls that new investors face.

To illustrate how we might want to position our stock investment strategy going forward, we can discuss an example. Imagine that we have a buffer of $200 per month that we would like to invest, and we've determined that these funds aren't needed soon. Therefore, we can explore stock investments. You might think that $200 per month isn't enough to get started. Before the advent of fintech apps, you would be correct in saying that you need more capital to make it worth your while. Years ago, you needed to pay commissions per trade, sometimes upwards of $10 per transaction. In 2020, there are several phone apps that you can use to get started with investing, and these apps are intended to be cost-friendly options for retail investors. Two that come to mind are Stash and Robinhood. For ease of use, I prefer Stash, though they do charge a small fee for their service. Stash allows you to pick your favorite companies, set an investment amount, and start contributing right away. Their auto-invest system schedules withdrawals from your bank account into your investment account, so there's no need to worry about forgetting to invest in a particular month. You can also tailor the investment schedule to fit your needs, as some people like the idea of weekly or biweekly investments. If you're more focused on picking individual stocks, Robinhood allows fractional share purchases and is perhaps the most popular investing app for investing newcomers. These apps often include the most popular companies in the US, such as Amazon, Facebook, and Apple, among many others. I know several people who use these apps and are happy with the low fees and the ease with which they can schedule contributions.

Going back to our example, we can use investing apps to help us create a portfolio and schedule contributions that fit into our financial picture. If we determined that we could set aside $200 per month to invest, we can arrange an auto-investment through these apps and pick a few companies that we like. You might think that determining the amount to invest is more straightforward than is identifying the stocks we should choose, but it doesn't have to be complicated to start. We can keep it simple and select three to five companies whose products or services we enjoy using. For myself, this sort of list would look something like this:

1) Facebook, because I enjoy using the product and believe that the company still has a long runway for growth (especially when considering the potential of WhatsApp and Oculus).
2) Target, because I've always had a positive experience in their stores, and they always seem to stay ahead of the curve concerning e-commerce and customer satisfaction.
3) Amazon, because their customer service is exceptional, and they've proven successful in entering different product markets.

Once we have our shortlist, we can set up our portfolio to comprise these three to five stocks. We can also set the dollar amount we would like to purchase per period. Based on the price per share at the time of the contribution, you might be buying more or less shares when compared to a previous period. These apps will perform all calculations for you, so you only need to concern yourself with the dollar amount and not the share quantities. This is a fundamental concept that has applications for retail investors, one that Burton Malkiel wrote about extensively in his work "A Random Walk Down Wall Street." He discusses the concept of investing the same sum of money every period, regardless of stock prices or current market movements. This idea has blossomed into the phrase "Dollar Cost Averaging," which has become one of the most popular investing strategies in the world. Its simplicity and viability over the long-term have contributed to its rising popularity. One benefit of Dollar Cost Averaging (or DCA) is that you will be buying shares of your favorite companies on a consistent schedule.

Regardless of whether share prices are high or low, you will be purchasing shares in equally spaced intervals. This plan takes the guesswork out of determining whether today is a good day to buy, or whether tomorrow will be even better. Another benefit of this framework is that it dramatically reduces the emotional tug-of-war that often arises while investing. Instead of buying at one price and potentially second-guessing our decision later, we give ourselves the flexibility to buy at multiple prices on multiple days. If the share price decreases in the interim, we are buying more shares at lower prices, which should make us happy if we are still fans of the company. Conversely, if the share price increases, our current holdings will increase in value as well. This outcome will also make us happy because our goal is to own assets that will appreciate in value and compensate us for taking risks. There is give and take on both sides, but it's easy to see the benefits of DCA and how it can help budding investors get started while simultaneously stripping emotions out of the equation.

For our model portfolio, we would be buying all three stocks for a total contribution of $200 per period. Our last step lies in determining the amount of funds we will dedicate to each company. If you're the most confident in a particular company, you can allocate more funds in that direction. I can say for myself that, out of the three companies I listed, I am most confident in Facebook's potential to continue its dominance within social media. It's a good idea to weigh your position sizing based on your confidence in each company's future success. As an example, I can allocate $100 to Facebook, $50 to Target, and $50 to Amazon. In one year, I will contribute $1,200 to Facebook, $600 to Target, and $600 to Amazon, for a total yearly contribution of $2,400. You can set yourself up in a similar manner, and you don't have to stick with precisely three companies or exactly $200 per month. Of course, these choices will be up to you to make. I've provided these examples here to give you some ideas about how you can proceed into a new chapter, one in which you start thinking about playing offense with your finances. If this frame of mind is different for you, please don't fret. I didn't start thinking in this manner until recently, but it has helped keep my financial life balanced between measured conservatism and opportunistic aggressiveness. In my view, conservatism is necessary to build a buffer into your monthly budget. Opportunistic aggressiveness is needed to accelerate the growth of assets. Having a two-pronged strategy can help you diversify capital between defensive instruments (such as cash) and offensive instruments (such as stocks).

We spoke about compound interest in a previous paragraph and its importance in growing wealth. We also discussed using our $200 per month buffer to buy stocks with some regularity. I would like to combine these two concepts to show how powerful compounding can be when we put capital to work effectively. If we were to invest $200 per month for 5 years, we would contribute a total of $12,000. If our investment grows by 7% per year, the value of our investment at the end of 5 years would be $14,239.17. Our total interest earned would be the difference between the amount we contributed and the final amount of the investment, or $2,239.17. This difference becomes more pronounced as we increase our investment's time horizon. If we kept everything the same as the previous example, except we lengthened our horizon to 10 years, we would have contributed a total of $24,000. The future value of our investment would be $34,210.35, and the total interest earned would be $10,210.35. We used 7% as an exemplary growth rate because the S&P 500 Index has historically returned higher than this figure over the long-term (somewhere around 9% to 10%, depending on the period used). You can see here that consistent investments, paired with compound growth, can lead to the organic growth of your assets over time. Perhaps the operative point is that we didn't need material startup capital to achieve gains exceeding $10,000 over ten years. Instead, we simply needed to focus on consistently adding to our investments and pick investments that give us the best chance for sustainable growth. Conveniently, the investment apps mentioned previously will take care of automatic contributions, so our only concern is to pick investments that will grow our funds.

Each person will have their own level of confidence as to whether they can succeed in picking individual stocks. If you are confident that you can pick stocks which will appreciate in price over your time horizon, then you should do some research, pick a few companies as we mentioned, set a defined contribution schedule, and let it be. However, some people aren't sure if they can choose the right stocks. Others simply don't have the time or don't want to make the time required to conduct due diligence on individual companies.

Over the last few decades, institutions created a few financial instruments to serve those who want to buy stocks without needing to pick specific companies. These two investment funds are called ETFs and Mutual Funds. ETF is an acronym for Exchange-Traded Funds. Investopedia defines ETFs as follows: "An exchange-traded fund (ETF) is a type of security that involves a collection of securities—such as stocks—that often tracks an underlying index, although they can invest in any number of industry sectors or use various strategies." An ETF will often track an index composed of multiple stocks. For example, there are several S&P 500 index funds, all of which have ETFs available. These funds can track the whole index, specific sectors within the index, or different segments (called factors) such as value stocks or growth stocks. Mutual funds are similar, except they often have a different tax structure and are sometimes actively managed. Active management means that fund managers will try to outperform an index instead of merely tracking an index. ETFs are also a bit nimbler and allow for quick pricing execution during the trading day. In contrast, mutual funds aren't adequately designed for trading in and out quickly. Since many investment apps allow you to buy fractional shares of securities, I think ETFs accomplish the job well and allow the most flexibility. Also, ETFs will often charge lower fees than their mutual fund counterparts because their passive nature requires less expenditure for the administrating companies.

We can set our portfolio up to include individual stocks, ETFs, and mutual funds in any combination of our choosing. If you like the idea of buying shares of smaller companies, there are many ETFs and mutual funds that will invest in those companies. Conversely, if you prefer investing in big companies, you'll find no shortage of funds that will help you fine-tune your portfolio to this preference. This idea also applies to the geographic, sector, or other relevant factors you can consider.

One exciting point about starting your journey right now is that the options available to you are substantially more numerous than those available to investors before the 1990s. The final decade of the last millennium brought many changes to the forefront, including online stock trading, reduced commissions, and products such as ETFs and low-cost mutual funds. A famous saying states that there's no better time than today to start something new, and that is especially true in regards to personal finance and investing. I encourage you to explore apps and companies that will help make your financial life more manageable. We already have enough stressors, so why not try to make processes streamlined and automated where we can? Ease of use is something that I will be emphasizing throughout this text. Improving your financial health doesn't need to be complicated. It should be our collective goal to put our best foot forward in the simplest way possible.

Let's recap what we learned in this chapter:

- We learned about stock investments, what they represent, and their importance in helping us grow wealth.
- We further examined compound interest, how it differs from simple interest, and we posited an example which showed its power in growing wealth.
- We learned how to set up a portfolio and how we can start choosing stocks today without spending hours conducting research (if we so choose).
- We learned about ETFs and mutual funds, which are funds available to investors who want to diversify risk by investing in multiple stocks at once. Using these products can help us accommodate our sector, factor, or size needs.

I'm excited for you to start investing. Many people find participating in the market to be somewhat intimidating. However, it can be gratifying in multiple ways. You're looking to grow your assets first and foremost. We would expect nothing less. Besides offering an opportunity to grow your assets, the market is an avenue through which you will learn about business, world affairs, and investor psychology. For myself, it has contributed more to my knowledge of the world than perhaps any other source I've encountered. You can be as involved or as passive as you'd like, and you can still be a successful investor and accomplish your goals without dedicating your life to investing. With less than half of U.S. households currently owning stocks, there is tremendous opportunity to jump into the markets and become not only wealthier but also more educated and more knowledgeable about the world around you.

In the next chapter, we will examine student loans, their characteristics, and how we can devise an appropriate payment plan to emerge on the other side victorious!

Chapter 4: Student Loans

I originally wanted to start this chapter by detailing the statistics about student loans. After some thought, I felt it was best to talk for a minute about the psychological aspect of this issue. For many current and former college grads, dealing with loan payments can be daunting. It's easy to become intimidated when looking at a large balance, even if your monthly payments are manageable. It is important to stress here that you will make it through to the other side. It might be difficult to stay motivated, but I implore you to try your best. Trust me when I say that you are not the only one dealing with this issue. You will conquer this one day at a time. Now, on to the numbers.

Student loans have become the most important financial issue of the 21st century for millions of Americans. For the most recent graduating Class of 2019, 69% of college students borrowed using student loans. The average debt upon graduation summed up to just under $30,000. This fact doesn't even count the 14% of parents who took out an average of $37,200 in federal parent PLUS loans. In total, U.S. student loan borrowers owe over $1.64 trillion in debt, spread out over about 45 million borrowers. If we took the average debt balance at graduation and prorated it to a ten year loan period, we see that the payment is north of $300 per month. As much as the topic has become mainstream, there is still no cohesive plan to deal with the problem on a national level.

I've dedicated an entire chapter of this text to the topic of student loans because I believe it deserves much attention. The truth is that, to stay competitive in 2020 and beyond, most people feel a college degree is necessary. For those looking to join the professional world, many think that college is a requirement, a mandatory right of passage needed to achieve their dreams. While some employers have recently started to remove the long-standing degree requirement, high school seniors largely still see college as the best way forward. Of course, trade schools and civil service/government jobs are still an option and will always need to recruit new candidates.

Government policies, coupled with better awareness from future prospective college students, could help bridge the gap in the future. However, digressing into how future generations can solve the current student debt crisis won't do much to improve your situation. Uncovering the mindset needed to succeed, along with devising an actionable plan to place ourselves on the path to success, are both much better strategies. We will start by examining the different characteristics of student loans.

It's important to understand that there are two categories of student loans: federal and private. Federal student loans and federal parent loans are owned by the government. In contrast, private student loans are made by a lender such as a bank, credit union, state agency, or a school. Federal loans are made directly by the government and often operate within the restrictions set by law. As a result, borrowers are usually granted fixed interest rates and are given the option of an income-driven repayment plan. These benefits are included to incentivize borrowers and to provide them protection. There are a few different types of federal loans, and I would like to dedicate a subsection to each type of loan. If you are a future college student, it is imperative that you fully understand the distinctions between federal loans. Likewise, if you are a current student or a college graduate (congratulations!), you will want to know your loan 'like the back of your hand.'

Direct Subsidized Loans

Direct Subsidized Loans are perhaps the most popular option for student loan borrowers. These loans are widely available to students who demonstrate financial need (these loans are only available to undergraduate students). This type of loan has better terms than does its unsubsidized counterpart. The school you attend will often set the borrowing limit for this type of loan. However, the U.S. Department of Education does set their own maximum for borrowers as well. The limit starts at $3,500 per year and increases by $1,000 per year for each year you attend school up to your third year. The limit is capped at $5,500 after your third year. One of the most significant benefits of subsidized loans is that the government will pay the interest on the loan in any of the following three cases:

- During any period where you are considered at least half-time in credits taken (generally 6 to 8 credit-hours).
- During the first six months after graduation (referred to as a "grace period").
- During any period of deferment, which is a temporary postponement of loan payments.

If you need to take out a loan to pay for school, Direct Subsidized Loans should be where you look first. If you demonstrated financial need during the borrowing process, you most likely have a Direct Subsidized Loan. In case you're unsure, it's a good idea to check this on your borrower portal. This information should have been given to you before your grace period ended.

The maximum period for which you can borrow a Direct Subsidized Loan is 150 percent of the published time to complete your specific school program. For example, if you plan on attending a 4-year degree, you are allowed up to 6 years of eligibility for a Direct Subsidized Loan. After this point, you are still eligible for other types of loans (namely Direct Unsubsidized Loans and Direct PLUS Loans). Nevertheless, your time to use Direct Subsidized Loans will eventually run out. There are, of course, several reasons why you might want to finish school as early as possible, but please do keep this in mind if you are either a prospective or current college student.

The interest rates for Direct Subsidized Loans are more reasonable than that of private loans, with the applicable rate for the 2019-2020 school year coming in at 4.53%. This information can be found on the FSA website and can change year-to-year based on prevailing interest rates. This rate is fixed for the life of the loan, which is a plus for recent borrowers as rates have been declining slowly for several decades, leading to lower interest costs for graduates.

To get a sense of how changes in the total amount borrowed will change the total amount paid, we can look at several scenarios. This exercise could be especially useful for someone who is aiming to attend college soon but is concerned about how the finances will factor into the equation. For those of you who have already graduated, it is helpful to see how the final output can change based on the inputs used.

Let's start by introducing our example individual: Student A. She's a well-rounded student and currently has an interest in marketing. She decides that her local state school can fulfill her needs, so she matriculates into SUNY Binghamton. Since she grew up within an hour's drive of the school, she plans on commuting to school come fall semester. This plan saves her $16,000 per year in housing and food costs. Even if we assume that she spends $4,000 on food during the school year, commuting would still save her $12,000 per year, or $48,000 in total for the four years. We can run two scenarios:

- Student A commutes to Binghamton and takes out several Direct Subsidized Loans for an interest rate of 4.53% and a total principal of $40,000 ($10,000 per year).
- Student A lives on campus and takes out several Direct Subsidized Loans for an interest rate of 4.53% and a total principal of $88,000 ($22,000 per year).

We can use loan payment calculators to compute the monthly payment amount for both cases (I prefer Bankrate's calculator). We will assume a 10-year repayment schedule, which is the schedule used for the majority of today's student loans. Let's open up a loan payment calculator and input the following variables for the first scenario:

- Loan Amount of $40,000.
- Interest Rate of 4.53%.
- Duration of 120 months.

Under the parameters of the first scenario, Student A's monthly payment would be $415.13 per month for the duration of the loan. The total interest paid would equal $9,815.88, so the total payment altogether would equal just under $50,000. If she pays a higher monthly amount, the duration of her loan will decrease, as would the total interest paid. Conversely, her monthly payments would increase (as would the interest) if she were to pay less than $415.13 per month. As mentioned, the U.S. Department of Education will waive accruing interest for both your grace period after graduation and during any loan deferment period. As such, these two periods won't increase your monthly payment.

Under the parameters of the second scenario, Student A's monthly payment would be $913.29. The only difference is that the Loan Amount for the second scenario will be $88,000 because we are assuming she will live on campus. When comparing the monthly payments, we see that her choosing to live on campus would result in an additional burden of approximately $500 per month. This monthly payment would not only be difficult to justify, but it would constrain her post-college future as well. By stripping away valuable cash savings, she will have more difficulty building her asset base over time. As mentioned in our chapter regarding Budgeting, we should be thinking of loans as liabilities. Every dollar paid to a creditor is one less dollar that you can save in cash or invest in the market. Hence, the ramifications of the college decision persist longer than the attending of college itself.

The extra $500 per month we highlighted could make a substantial difference in post-college financial standing. If Student A chose the first scenario, she would have an additional $500 per month that she would not have if she chose the second scenario. If she took this incremental $500 per month and invested it for ten years at a 7% rate of return per year, the final balance at the end of ten years would be $85,525.87. Total contributions would equal $60,000, and total capital gains (interest) would equal $25,525.87. This example is meant to show the power of compound interest.

You can think of this idea as opportunity cost, where taking out large loans for college can have a bigger or smaller opportunity cost, depending on your outlook. One could make the argument that the 'college experience' of living on campus during those four years is worth more than the amount of money you could earn through investments after school. I think the best choice for you can only come from a combination of your heart and your brain. In life, we are sometimes faced with decisions that pit logical reasoning (our brain) with emotions (our heart). It will be up to you to determine whether something is worth doing, as only you can decide if you will be happy in any given situation. I know some people who went away to college, many of whom had a great time. Others didn't mind commuting from home and were able to save money in the process. I aim to inform you about how your college decision can affect your life in several facets, not just financially. As much as this text focuses on personal finances, money is not the only important thing in life.

Getting back to Direct Subsidized Loans, we see that they have several benefits we want to exploit. Let's take a look at Direct Unsubsidized Loans and their general characteristics, advantages, and disadvantages.

Direct Unsubsidized Loans

As mentioned, Direct Unsubsidized Loans offer slightly worse terms for student borrowers than their Subsidized counterparts. The main downside to Unsubsidized Loans is that interest accrues while you attend college, resulting in increased interest costs compared to a Subsidized Loan of the same type. For undergraduate borrowers, the most recent interest rate for these loans is equivalent to the rate on Subsidized Loans (4.53% during the 2019-2020 school year). For graduate borrowers, the interest rate increases to 6.08%. Even with interest rates being relatively low, allowing the interest to accrue for four years can add a substantial amount to the starting balance (and, consequently, the monthly payment). In our first scenario with Student A, her monthly payment upon graduation would increase from $415.13 to $495.62 if she were to borrow using Unsubsidized Loans as opposed to Subsidized Loans (an increase of $80.49). Her balance grows at a rate of 4.53% per year for the four years of college. This growth doesn't happen with Direct Subsidized Loans because the U.S. Department of Education pays the interest on the loan while you attend school.

As a result, Direct Unsubsidized Loans will always be a worse financial deal than Direct Subsidized Loans.

However, there are some positive aspects of unsubsidized loans, of which we should be aware. There is no financial need requirement to qualify for financial aid from unsubsidized loans, so you need not be worried about qualifying for this type of loan. It's good to know that you have options in case you don't qualify for the subsidized version. Additionally, there is no restriction on the period for which you can borrow using unsubsidized loans. When compared with the 150% requirement of subsidized loans, this bodes well for students who take longer to finish school for a multitude of reasons. This type of loan also has higher borrowing limits than does the subsidized version, so you have more leeway in this department. Finally, since subsidized loans are not available to graduate or professional students, Direct Unsubsidized Loans seem to be the next best option for those who fit into these groups.

We've now covered the two most popular options for student borrowers, which are grouped as Federal Direct Loans. There are two other (less popular) types of Federal Direct Loans available to borrowers. Lastly, students can opt to borrow using private student loans, which are more personalized but also more expensive in the long run. In the interest of being thorough, I'll be presenting a concise synopsis of the remaining options to students who need help paying for college. Following that, we'll discuss different repayment strategies to help you manage your current debt load.

Direct PLUS Loans

Direct Plus Loans can be made to either parents of grad students or grad students themselves. This type of loan is often used to bridge the gap between the full cost of attendance and all other financial aid received. The maximum amount allowed to be borrowed is the difference between the cost of attendance and all other financial aid received. The current interest rate for both PLUS Loans is 7.08%, which is the highest rate among federal loans. On these loans, interest works the same way as with unsubsidized loans, where interest accrues and adds to your balance while you're in school. Less-than-stellar credit may make obtaining these loans more difficult than others, though the government will make exceptions in some cases. Overall, a PLUS Loan seems to be a good option for those who might not be eligible for the subsidized or unsubsidized loans. It also works for those who have exceeded the borrowing limits for those two types of loans.

Direct Consolidation Loans

Direct Consolidation Loans are a handy tool that can help you combine your outstanding student loans into one loan. Consolidation means that, instead of making multiple payments per month and complicating the budget, you can fuse them into one simple monthly payment. This process often results in a longer loan duration. If you choose to pay only the monthly minimum, you might incur higher interest costs than you would if you decided not to consolidate in the first place. For budgeting purposes, we'll want to make things as simple as possible, and a Direct Consolidation Loan might help you accomplish this and make your life easier. If you currently have multiple student loans and you find it to be a hassle, consider this option and determine whether it simplifies your life.

Private Student Loans

Before we look at different strategies for paying off these pesky loans, we should review the last option for student loan borrowers, which is private student loans. These loans don't have the same uniformity seen in federal loans, so making generalizations is a bit difficult. We can broadly say a few things about private loans in comparison to federal loans:

- Many private loans require payments while you're still in school, but some do allow deferment.
- Private loans are likely going to involve higher interest rates than comparable federal loans. These

- higher rates persist because lenders will be accounting for your lack of credit and income history when determining loan terms.
- Interest will often be due for all periods, as subsidized private loans are rare.
- Substantially all private loans will require a credit check, which can be a barrier for those with adverse credit history.

In sum, private student loans should be your last resort when deciding how to pay for college. While they are more customizable than are federal loans, you will rarely get equal or better terms when compared to federal loans. You are very likely to qualify for some level of federal aid, so your best bet is to exhaust all possible federal aid first. Once you've done this, then you can look to use private loans.

Hopefully, the preceding summary helped you understand the different types of loans available to college students. If you've already graduated from college, I'm sure this knowledge will prove useful in the future if you decide to have kids and they are aiming for college. The thought of figuring out college costs, which loans to use, and whether you can swing certain costs causes great distress to many people. It's great that you are looking to learn more about student loans and how you can use different strategies to help you deal with the debt load. There are five strategies that I would like you to consider: dedicated second job, avalanche method, snowball method, reducing expenses, and using microsaving apps.

Dedicated Second Job

Getting a second job and earning some extra cash can help you pay off your student loans quicker. I understand that most people are busy as it is, so this might not work with everyone's schedule. However, with the rise of the gig economy, it's easier than ever to start driving for Uber, delivering for Doordash or writing blog articles for publication websites. This job doesn't have to be a time sink to make a difference in your life. If you earned $10 an hour while working an extra 5 hours per week, you could potentially pay an additional $200 per month on your loans. This $200 would undoubtedly make a dent in your loan balance. The key here is that, preferably, all income from this second job would be directed towards paying off debt. If you allow yourself to view it as "fun money," you might have a tougher time separating the two when it's time to pay your bills. Mental accounting may seem silly, but it does seem to be a good strategy for handling the mental aspect of allocating dual incomes. Depending on your hobbies, you could also turn one of your hobbies into a side business. I know multiple people who took to Etsy and other marketplace websites to sell decorated goods. Perhaps you already babysit or dogsit for a friend and earn extra cash. Please don't be afraid to work this idea into your budget and overall strategy. If your current monthly payment is $300 per month, and you earn $300 per month on the side, you can pay $600 per month and pay off the loan much faster.

As an example, we could have a ten-year loan at 4.53% with a starting balance of $30,000 (close to the average student loan debt coming out of school). Our monthly payment would come out to $311.35. If we were able to earn an extra $300 per month and put these funds directly to the loan, we would pay off the loan within five years and save over $4,000 in interest costs. This powerful example shows how doing just a little bit every day to help yourself will add up over time and compound in its own way. This strategy can also be combined with other initiatives. There's no need to feel like your only option is to obtain a second job and work longer hours. Depending on your willingness and ability to take more time out of your schedule, I do think this option is worth considering because you'll be working towards a defined goal. This ultimate objective should motivate you and help keep you on the desired path. It can be hard to achieve objectives when we can't see the end goal. Feel free to keep these mental aspects in mind going forward, as they play a substantial role in both success and personal development.

Avalanche Method

The second strategy we'll examine is the avalanche

method, which we briefly discussed in the Budgeting chapter. This method involves targeting our funds towards loans with the highest interest rates. If we have four loans with four different interest rates, we would first make the standard payment for each loan every month. Then, we would allocate any extra funds to the loan with the highest interest rate. This strategy saves the most money in interest costs over the long run because it knocks out the highest interest loans first. The total loan balance has no bearing on the avalanche method. Regardless of any other loan characteristics, we are allocating any extra funds to the loans that come with the highest interest rate.

A common criticism of the avalanche method is that it can be challenging to stay motivated. Studies have shown that tackling smaller balances first (and subsequently closing debt accounts) has predicted success in future debt elimination. The benefits of the avalanche method might not be as evident to you because this method doesn't prioritize closing smaller accounts first and building up mental confidence. From a purely mathematical standpoint, this strategy is superior to other debt repayment methods, but this doesn't mean that we should only use this method. If you think you'd benefit from honing in on smaller debt balances first, you might be interested in the snowball method. As with the avalanche method, we touched on the snowball method within the context of budgeting, so I will give you a quick synopsis of its benefits and drawbacks.

Snowball Method

The snowball method, as with the avalanche method, necessitates paying the minimum monthly payments for each loan as the first step. From there, we rank our different loans based on the outstanding balances remaining. We then begin to attack the loan with the lowest balance remaining. Every extra dollar we can reasonably spare (after accounting for an emergency fund) will be thrown at this loan, in an attempt to kill it as quickly as possible. Once we defeat the first loan, we move on to the loan with the next-lowest balance. By way of example, say we have three 10-year loans as follows:

- Loan A has a balance of $5,000 and an interest rate of 3%.
- Loan B has a balance of $10,000 and an interest rate of 5%.
- Loan C has a balance of $15,000 and an interest rate of 7%.

If we were to follow the avalanche method, we would be focusing on first paying off Loan C, then Loan B, then finally Loan A. Loan C has the highest interest rate of 7%, followed by B with 5% and A with 3%. To reiterate, this will mathematically save us more in interest costs than the snowball method. However, the snowball method has a tremendous advantage in the psychological effect it has on borrowers. As mentioned, this is why Dave Ramsey is such a huge proponent of this debt repayment strategy. We start by ranking our debts in order of balance outstanding. Thankfully, the above list needs no further organization. After making all minimum payments, we target Loan A. Once we knock this loan out, we will shift focus to Loan B. This process continues until we are done paying our loans.

As with much of personal finance, there is not a "one size fits all" answer to student loan repayment. Analytical people might be more inclined to try the avalanche method due to its inherent mathematical advantage. In contrast, others might gravitate towards the snowball method and benefit from tackling one loan at a time. The snowball method seems to bring the most applicability to the largest segment of borrowers, especially those of whom have been struggling with debt and need help staying motivated throughout the process. If you can imagine yourself feeling accomplished and driven after closing a loan account, the snowball method could be a great fit for you.

Now that we've seen the two most popular debt repayment strategies, I'll talk about how you can reduce expenses and sprinkle this into your financial plan.

Reducing Expenses

Reducing expenses is an indirect action which, if implemented correctly, should increase the amount of funds available with which you can pay your student loans. If you can currently allocate a maximum of $300 per month to debt repayments, you could increase this to $400 per month if you're able to cut your expenses by $100 per month. Popular ideas for reducing costs include making coffee at home, purchasing generic brands in stores, and cooking your own food. If you grab coffee or drinks often, try cutting your consumption in half. Going from 5 cups per week to 2 per week could save you $10 per week (or about $40 per month). Small measures like this can be combined with other actions, and you'll quickly see that even modest efforts can lead to outstanding results.

The idea of cutting expenses can sometimes raise eyebrows because few people are excited to cut spending in areas such as coffee, hobbies, or other entertainment categories. Thankfully, substantial positive impacts often do not require drastic changes. As we highlighted with the coffee example, modest habit shifts can do great things for us over time. We also touched on this idea when discussing investing. In the context of our lives, the impact of a short-lived habit shift doesn't compare to the result of positive lifestyle developments. Think of how people try fad diets. While those quick-hitting changes in food choices will often lead to short-term weight loss, we often see people struggling to keep the weight off after the initial burst. Those folks would probably be better served by thinking about their current lifestyle and comparing it to the lifestyle they want to live. Lastly, they can consider how they can modify their current habits to help themselves going forward. We need to think in terms of months and years instead of mere weeks. Making a rapid transition from always eating out to never eating out would make anyone go stir-crazy, and I'm sure the opposite is true as well.

One strategy to consider involves slashing expenditures on big-ticket items first. For example, reducing a $2,000 rent expense by 10% would save you $200 per month. This action could be more feasible than trying to completely remove categories such as dining out or streaming services. Your strategy will depend on your personal goals and proclivities, but I do think that starting with larger expenses first can help you greatly.

If you're interested in learning more about how habits

form and how we can shape them, I would recommend picking up a copy of *Atomic Habits* by James Clear. Gaining a better understanding of yourself is always worthwhile, and framing your mannerisms as part of your lifestyle can help you make a change and stick with it. Clear's book gave me great insight into how habits form over time and how we can shift our thinking to shape them positively.

Microsaving Apps

The final debt repayment strategy we will note here is microsaving. Before computers, the internet, and smartphones, people needed to take measured steps to save money. Common tricks of the time included placing dollar bills in jars, stuffing cash in envelopes, or making frequent trips to the bank. In some capacity, these actions are still taken today. However, with the technology we have at our disposal, we have options that people before us could only dream of having. Our best path forward involves using this technology to help us achieve our goals. For student loan repayments, one way we can do this is by using microsaving apps. These programs will round-up your purchases to the nearest dollar and invest or save the difference within a separate bank account. One of the most popular examples of microsaving apps is Acorns, which has now grown to over 3.5 million customers. These apps typically take a small fee for their service, which can amount to approximately $1 per month. An illustrative example works like this: You buy a coffee for $3.50 with your credit card. These apps will calculate the difference between your purchase and the next whole dollar amount (which, in this case, is $0.50). They will then transfer this calculated amount from your connected checking account to a savings account. At that point, the money can either be kept in cash or invested in various assets. The beauty of this process is that it requires no effort on your part. Your funds will continue to grow over time, especially if you can take advantage of compounding your funds through gains in the stock market.

Acorns is a great app for folks who are looking to bulk up their savings. It has great utility for those who want to save first and allocate later. However, student loan payments are not the main focus of Acorns. This is where ChangEd comes into play. ChangEd is an app that implements a similar round-up feature to Acorns. However, when your savings balance reaches $100, the app will send the money as a payment to your student loans. This feature helps automate the student loan process and allows you to make your minimum payments manually while adding extra funds through microsaving. Using ChangEd, you'll knock out your loans in a shorter amount of time than solely paying the minimum per month. You can also boost your savings by making additional deposits, which will shorten the amount of time until you reach the $100 threshold. I highly recommend checking out this service, which was previously featured on Shark Tank and subsequently funded by Mark Cuban.

Now that we've talked about the different types of student loans, their characteristics, and how we can use repayment strategies to help ourselves, let's recap the key takeaways:

- We looked at four types of federal loans (Subsidized, Unsubsidized, Parent PLUS, and Consolidated). Our analysis of loan characteristics confirmed the idea that Subsidized loans are the best option for borrowers.
- We examined private loans and compared the general benefits and drawbacks between private and federal loans. We were not able to find any benefits of private loans, so we recommend that we try to avoid them whenever feasible.
- On the repayment side, we aim to approach the issue from multiple angles (increasing income and decreasing expenses). We can break down student loan repayment strategies into two methods: the avalanche method and the snowball method. Avalanche is more mathematically sound, whereas snowball plays to our psyche.
- We also researched useful phone apps that can help automate the process and reduce our repayment

duration.

Student debt is a growing problem in America, and I hope that you can leverage your existing assets and knowledge to conquer this issue on a personal level. By combining your motivation to succeed with the strategies and tools given here, you have put yourself in a very favorable position. I commend you for bettering yourself in this arena because too many people with untapped potential quit before they even get started. In the next chapter, I would like to finish discussing debt by targeting credit cards, auto loans, and mortgages.

Chapter 5: Credit Card, Auto Loan, and Mortgage Debts

In our quest to build a comprehensive personal finance framework, we touched on liabilities within both the Budgeting and Student Loan chapters. We can now round out the pie by discussing several of the most relevant types of consumer debt, which are credit cards, auto loans, and mortgages. When combined with student loans, these categories represent $14.3 trillion of U.S. debt, and you'll need to understand how these liabilities work to use them properly. Contrary to popular belief, borrowing money can be advantageous in certain situations. Accordingly, we'll want to understand the benefits of these debt vehicles and their implementation within our system. To continue in order, we can start with credit cards.

Credit Cards

Simply put, credit cards allow you access to a small line of credit that you can use to purchase goods and services. These cards operate on a monthly cycle, where you will have a "statement ending date" every month. You need to make at least the minimum payment each month, which is usually a fraction of the total balance due. If you fail to make the minimum payment, your credit score could suffer, or the terms given by your bank could worsen. Unfortunately, our dear friend named interest is back to dampen our plans! As long as you allow a given balance to be kept past the statement due date, interest will accrue on that balance. In our previous descent into interest rates and compounding, we were working with interest rates generally lower than 10%. I hope you're sitting down for this next bit because it could knock you off your feet: interest rates on credit cards can vary between 20% to 30%! The midpoint of this range is approximately five times the average federal student loan rate. As an example, if you let a balance of $100 grow at a rate of 25% for one year, you would end up owing $125 at the end of the year. This further compounds against you (and in favor of your bank) the longer you keep the balance alive. To illustrate a further example: imagine we have a credit card balance of $5,000 and an APR (Annual Percentage Rate) of 25%. If we decide that we want to pay off the loan within 12 months, we will make monthly payments of $513. However, if we instead made the minimum monthly payment (assuming a minimum of $200), we would make monthly payments of $200, and we would be paying the loan for a duration of 36 months (or three years). This exercise underscores the degree to which compounding takes place on high-interest credit cards. I'm sure it is clear how falling behind on your credit card payments can set you back financially.

  I remember the process of obtaining my first credit card well. When I was 18 years old, I became interested in building credit. At the same time, I noticed friends and family using cards and thought it would be nice to have a more secure method of payment. Up until this time, I had only been using cash and debit cards to pay for goods and services. Using credit seemed to be the next logical step in the progression of my financial life. My mother and I took a ride to the local bank branch. Here, we spoke to a representative who walked us through the process of applying for a card. Since I was applying for a student card, I didn't need to show a significant income to receive approval. After approval, the bank gave me a monthly limit of $300. My limit was then raised to $500 after about six months of steady payments. Nowadays, this process can be done entirely online from start to finish. However, I think that first-time cardholders will gain a lot of knowledge and comfort from speaking to someone at a branch. The representative can help answer questions and assuage any concerns you might have. Once you become more experienced, completing further applications online should be both sufficient and effective.

  A comprehensive view of credit cards should involve both benefits and drawbacks, as it's not accurate to say that credit cards only have negative attributes. To help guide our analysis, I'll list the negatives first, and afterward, we can consider how credit cards can help us.

Drawbacks of Credit Cards

- Substantially all credit cards come with high interest rates, generally above 20%. We demonstrated the pitfalls of allowing balances to compound at high rates.
- Making late payments or going over your credit limit will likely damage your credit history. Poor credit history makes acquiring future loans more difficult and creates unfavorable loan terms for you.
- Having a credit line at your disposal might lead you to think you have more assets than you actually have. Using a credit line does free up cash in the short-term, but it is recorded as a liability on your balance sheet (for a business, this is represented as "Accounts Payable.")

Benefits of Credit Cards

- If used properly, credit cards can help you build good credit by establishing a history of timely payments. This history will be vital for you because receiving favorable terms from lenders going forward will help save you money in interest costs. If we fail to build a credit history, we can run into problems when applying for mortgages and other large loans (mortgages will be covered in detail soon).
- Banks offer many types of rewards cards for qualified individuals. For example, the Citi Double Cash card offers 1% cash back for purchases and 1% cash back when you pay for those purchases. This sums to a total cashback of 2%, which generally accrues within your account until it hits a minimum threshold. For most cards, you can choose several redemption options, including direct deposit, check, or statement credit (among others). As an example, if you spent $1,000 every month for 12 months (or $12,000 for the year), you would earn $240 in

rewards. Other standard awards include points, sign-on bonuses, and airline miles. Some cards, such as Chase Sapphire and Amex Platinum, have very competitive travel insurance structures. This incentive means that you won't need to pay for extra insurance when you buy plane tickets using these cards. For someone who travels often, this can be a nice plus.
- Credit cards offer flexibility for budgeting, and they grant protections to buyers that debit cards do not possess. If fraud occurs on your debit card, it will be a headache to remedy the situation because the money comes straight from your checking account. Conversely, if this happens on your credit card, the card issuer will freeze the card and help you resolve any disputes before any funds have been withdrawn. Credit cards are also safer because they add an extra layer between the card itself and the account from which the card is paid. This arrangement is different from that of debit cards, which link right to your checking account.
- Credit cards are incredibly convenient and will often take the place of holding a large number of cash bills. This convenience further applies when shopping for big-ticket items such as computers, televisions, or vacations.

Based on the above list, you can make the argument that credit cards can be either detrimental or advantageous to the user. Taking a look at scenarios where using a credit card makes sense can help us understand its best uses. Additionally, explaining solutions to the most common pitfalls and highlighting how we can stay conservative will save us interest costs (and headaches) in the long run. Finally, I can explain how I like to use credit cards to give you a sense of my personal strategy.

First, we should consider the relevant scenarios in which using a line of credit will benefit us. Credit cards can be great for bills that recur every month, such as Netflix or Amazon

Prime. These can easily be tracked within your budget and allows you to build up credit on an automated basis. Even if you don't use the card often, having some auto-purchases on your bill will help you establish credit going forward. It can be as little as a $10 Netflix subscription or a $20 magazine payment; as long as it recurs, your credit will build as you continue to pay.

Besides recurring payments, we'll want to explore the protections offered to us by credit cards. If you buy a $1,000 TV with cash or debit card, it can be a pain to process the refund if something goes wrong. However, if you were to buy this TV using a credit card, you will be protected. If something goes wrong, the issuer will either knock the charge off your statement or put the charge into dispute. These actions give you and the issuer time to resolve the issue before you pay the cost.

Similarly, if a product you ordered online is lost in the mail or is otherwise unable to be delivered, refunding other types of payments isn't always seamless. Since debit card payments come directly from your checking account, refunds can take a bit longer to process (usually 7 to 10 business days). Lastly, if cash is used to pay for a product for which there is an eventual refund, the vendor will often only be able to give "store credit." Store credit is similar to a gift card in that you can only use the credit at that particular store. Many young people who are getting their first cards find it hard to believe that using credit can be safer than using cash or debit. It's smart to understand the protections offered to us by using credit, even if it might feel scary at first.

Lastly, credit cards are good to have in case of emergencies. You might run into a situation where payday is coming up, but you have a bill to pay in the interim. If your money is predominately tied up elsewhere (such as stock investments or rental properties), swiping your card can give you more time to pay. In this sense, credit cards act as an insurance policy, but only if you plan to pay the balance before the statement due date. If you make a habit out of this practice, it might lead to debt accumulation, which is something we want to avoid at all costs on credit cards. As we've touched on before, debt can be useful and sometimes necessary in regard to big-ticket items such as college tuition and house purchases. With such high rates, credit cards will be the last place we want to accumulate any liabilities. If you have a current balance on your card that is accruing interest, I implore you to consider tackling this debt first with whatever funds you have available. Our previous examples showed the consequences of allowing high-interest rate credit cards to compound against you. It's essential to try your best to prevent such a problematic situation.

    Discussing some common pitfalls associated with hefty credit card use could help give you clarity on how to avoid these dilemmas. We've gone to great lengths in addressing the compounding of interest at rates above 20%. Potentially carrying a balance from month-to-month is the chief risk involved in using your card. If you are striving to practice solid money principles, it is in your best interest to only charge what you can pay before the statement due date. The statement balance is ordinarily due around 30 days after the statement end date. For example, the statement on my Citi Double Cash card ends on the 4th of the month, and the statement balance is due on the 1st of the following month. As an example, all charges between May 5th and June 4th would be due on July 1st. If you pay the full statement balance between June 4th and July 1st, your obligation will be satisfied, and you won't owe any interest. This process essentially gives you an interest-free loan from the time of purchase until the statement due date. The remaining balance on purchases between June 5th to July 4th would be due on August 1st.

    There is no obligation to pay the card down to zero every month. However, since I've started working full-time, I've adopted a strategy where I pay the entire current balance of the card at the end of the month. This plan works for me because I find it simpler to budget my funds this way. I can also run projections of future assets and liabilities fairly easily when I end the month with a card balance of zero. This strategy may not work for everyone, and some of you reading this might find it impractical or not feasible at the moment due to your situation. I believe it's important to share what works for me while also recognizing that this might not work for everyone equally. This approach might help you avoid the pitfall of carrying a month-to-month balance, especially when combined with the idea of limiting yourself to purchases you can pay off within the month.

Another risk inherent in credit card use is the risk that late payments will damage your credit history and result in difficulty with obtaining future loans. Negative marks against your credit history can signal to future lenders that lending to you is relatively riskier. This scenario will necessitate a higher interest rate or otherwise better terms for the lender. Your credit will continue to improve as long as you make the minimum payments every month, which is usually a small percentage of the balance due. Credit history will come into play if you ever decide to buy a house, so it's essential to consider the effects of today's decisions on tomorrow's situation. Simply put, having above-average credit will make your financial life more manageable and is one less thing to have on your plate.

It's good to note that having student loans and making the appropriate payments is positive for your credit history because student loans carry a long repayment period. The same goes for mortgages and car loans, though student loans carry a different purpose. You can frame this as similar to the job searching process. When looking for jobs, your experience in completing a task or demonstrating proficiency in achieving objectives can help others trust that you are competent in your field. This same logic can be applied to credit history, where lenders want to see that resume of accomplishments or experiences highlighting diligence and responsibility in making payments.

The last noteworthy downside involves consumer behavior. When we swipe our card for a purchase, no cash is taken from our wallets. Also, the transaction doesn't immediately affect our checking account as it does with a debit card. The nature of credit transactions might lead us to think that we have more money available to spend than is actually the case. Charging our card without keeping track of transactions could result in spending beyond our budgeted parameters. Overspending would undoubtedly lead to an unfortunate surprise when payment day comes around. This problem could more prominently affect new card users who are still wrapping their heads around the mechanics of credit cards. We can avoid this situation by comparing our current card balance against the remainder of our spending for the month. You don't need to track every purchase by hand, as your credit card's online portal does this for you automatically. However, anticipating upcoming expenses and determining whether our previous spending has exceeded our budget's expectations can tell us whether we need to reduce spending. We can also avoid this situation by training our brains to treat card swipes as cash coming out of your bank account. Try checking your card balance weekly and see if that helps you grasp the velocity and magnitude of your spending. You can cross-reference your card balance with your budget to make sure you're on track. For tracking purchases, cards beat cash, but I wouldn't you to overextend on the card side and hit your credit limit or run into other issues. In sum, keeping the psychological effect of credit card use in mind will keep you grounded.

So far, we've fleshed out the benefits and drawbacks of using credit cards. In doing this, I gave you some color as to my personal strategy with credit cards. Before summarizing our thoughts on credit cards here, I will delve into my personal credit strategy to give you ideas on how you can structure your credit card use going forward:

- For a given month, I estimate expenses (we should be doing this regardless of our credit status, but it's good to note here).
- Since income generally covers expenses and my credit limit is sufficiently high, I charge most monthly purchases to my card. The Citi Double Cash card maximizes my savings by giving me unlimited 2% cash back on all purchases, regardless of purchase type.
- I make sure to pay the entire current balance in full by the end of the month (as mentioned, my statement due date is the first of every month). I recognize that not everyone can afford this strategy and that it's not necessary to pay the current balance every month. The statement ending balance is the operative

payment amount for banks, and you won't earn a better credit score if you pay anything to the bank before it's due.

I like this strategy for myself because my total card balance resets every month. This reset allows for simplified budgeting as I don't need to keep a separate line item for credit card payments occurring in February stemming from purchases that occurred in January. If you plan on paying only the statement balance every month, you'll need to estimate this figure for each month based on your previous spending. In this case, your payment in February would be dependent on your purchases from January, plus any purchases from the start of February until the statement end date. In sum, you might need a dedicated line item if you plan to structure your payment around paying the statement balance.

Key takeaways regarding our chat on credit cards can be summarized as follows:

- Credit cards have both positives and negative aspects, and your goal will be to maximize positives earned and minimize negatives incurred simultaneously.
- For building credit, recurring monthly purchases are a great fit.
- Credit cards have inherent consumer protection features. Their ability to be used in an emergency is also a plus (but we will need to reserve this for true emergencies only).
- There are risks involved with using credit cards, such as potentially damaging your credit history and paying extra in interest costs.

Since we now have a better foothold on debt and liabilities, the next two subsections (covering auto loans and mortgages) should be lighter in nature. The following subsection will focus on auto loans.

Auto Loans

Cars represent one of the most significant purchases you'll make during your life. Since most people have a tough time paying for a car in full, obtaining financing is extremely popular with consumers. Without financing, you'd have to wait until you saved up the total amount of a car, which could mean saving for several months before starting the process. If you need a new car soon, it's unreasonable to save for 12 months until you accumulate enough to buy the car in full. When looking for a car loan, your options are twofold. You can either obtain a loan directly from a financial institution or get a loan through the auto dealership from which you are buying a car. You might be able to get better financing terms if you go through the bank or credit union, especially if you have a great relationship there. Also, since you're going directly to the bank for a loan, you should be paying lower fees than the alternative of going through the dealership. However, the drawback of using a bank is that it's a more complicated process. If you're looking for convenience, a dealer can act as a one-stop-shop. Dealerships can also procure loan offers from multiple banks, which saves you the hassle of going to numerous banks yourself and recording the different offers given. If you're looking for the most cost-effective option, calling your bank and asking how you can obtain a car loan is a good start. They should be able to provide you a quote based on the loan amount, duration, and credit history. If you're looking to save time, letting your dealer do the dirty work is your best bet, though you should understand that you'll be paying a premium because they are making a loan to you.

As with most consumer loans, several factors determine both the monthly payment and the lifetime cost. Your APR, or annual percentage rate, represents the fee you are paying to take out the loan. This rate will vary depending on your credit history, current macroeconomic conditions, and the risk practices of the lender. The down payment you choose will determine the amount needed as a loan. If you're able to put more cash down at the beginning, you will need to borrow less, and your monthly payment and lifetime cost will decrease accordingly. A typical rule-of-thumb is to pay at least 20% as a down payment. Though this is a fine target, if you can hit 25% or 30% instead, that would benefit you greatly. If you pay 20% down on a $20,000 car, you'd be borrowing $16,000. Conversely, a down payment of 30% would result in a loan of $14,000. The next chart illustrates these scenarios. Here, we see that increasing the down payment from 20% to 30% will decrease the monthly payment by about $35.

| Car Purchase of $20,000 (5% Interest Rate, 5-Year Term) ||||
Down Payment (%)	Down Payment ($)	Starting Loan Principal	Monthly Payment
20%	$4,000	$16,000	$301.94
30%	$6,000	$14,000	$264.20

Decreasing the amount you need to borrow will reduce your interest costs, though we should keep in mind that we never want to stretch ourselves too thin. The savings are even better for those who have poor credit and need to pay a higher interest rate as a result. Perhaps the most critical factor is the purchase price of the car. Only in the most extreme circumstances would a loan for a Honda Civic cost more than a loan for a Chevy Corvette. Finally, we have the loan term, which will generally vary between 36 months and 72 months (equivalent to three to six years). You'll notice that this term is shorter than the term on student loans, which is generally ten years in length.

The financial aspect of your loan can be summed up in two parts: the loan characteristics and the payoff structure. You can think of this model as an input-output where you have modest control over the input and substantial control over the output. The inputs into the loan are the characteristics we previously discussed. While you don't have full control over the terms given to you by any given bank, you can indirectly affect the input in three ways:

- You can do your best to practice good credit habits

and keep your credit score high.
- You can shop for loans from multiple banks to put yourself in the best position. Even if you take the same information to two banks, they might give you two different offers based on the risk evaluation processes they use.
- You can design a payment plan which will state the maximum you can afford to pay based on different inputs. If you'd prefer a shorter loan period, you might need to put more money down or be content with a lower purchase price on the car. Conversely, a more extended loan period would allow you to afford a higher purchase price, but you would be on the hook for a while and pay much more in both principal and interest costs. You can use affordability calculators to determine the maximum purchase price based on your target monthly payment, predicted interest rate, down payment, and loan duration. These calculators are available online.

It's preferable to refrain from maxing out your purchase price. Instead, try to aim for a payment that is 10% to 20% below the maximum purchase price feasible based on your parameters. If you've determined that your parameters and financial situation allow you to afford a maximum of $20,000, shooting for a car in the $16,000 to $18,000 range is good practice. This idea harkens back to one of the core principles we attempt to follow throughout our lives, which is living within our means.

Once we have our loan terms, we can start budgeting accordingly. We have full control over the payment of the loan (our "output" here), so we'll want to take full advantage by allocating funds to their best use. Two ways to hack this are as follows:

- Do your best to make extra payments when you can. If your job gives you a yearly bonus or you have a windfall from a tax refund, you can try to make one extra payment. Making one additional payment per year can help reduce your loan's duration. You could

potentially pay off a 5-year obligation in 4 to 4.5 years with this strategy.
- After you've been paying your loan for some time, you might earn raises at work or might otherwise have more ability to pay than at the outset of the loan. If this is the case, do your best to make monthly payments above the current payment amount. For example, increasing your payment from $500 to $550 (an increase of 10%) will do some extra damage to your remaining balance and will help you save on interest.

Combining both of these ideas can turn a 5-year loan into a 4-year affair without much hassle. Recognizing opportunities where you can take advantage of good fortune is the key to succeeding in most areas of life. This principle is especially relevant to personal finance. You will likely have opportunities where you can choose to allocate a portion to savings and a portion to spending, such as raises at work and inheritances passed down from family to you. Allocating $500 from a $5,000 raise to make an extra payment on your car loan might not seem to make a difference. However, you'd be surprised how impactful this action can be when combined with consistency and diligence. We can apply this idea to any time of debt payment, including student loans, credit cards, and mortgage loans.

Purchasing a car might lead to changes in your insurance rates. If you didn't already have comprehensive and collision coverage, your bank will likely require you to add this policy to your existing plan. Comprehensive coverage covers damages for incidents such as fires, vandalism, and inclement weather. Collision coverage covers damage to your car from an auto accident, regardless of fault. Trading in a car and subsequently purchasing a new vehicle might increase your rates because new car parts are more expensive to replace. Consider calling your insurance company if you're wondering how your new car purchase might affect your rates going forward.

Now that we've covered the basics of auto loans, we can

turn our attention to the final piece of the debt equation, which is the mortgage. Many interpretations of the American Dream have included homeownership as a core tenet. Whether you are innocent or experienced, young or old, you might be interested in owning a home in the future. Perhaps you already own a home and are looking for some guidance. A mortgage is often the most significant expense for most folks. Given this, we would be remiss not to elaborate on the specifics of how mortgages work and how we can budget accordingly.

Mortgages

Since we've become very familiar with other types of loans, mortgages shouldn't pose too much of a problem to understand. The process of buying a house is similar to that of buying a car, so the concepts are generally transferable. However, property will likely be the most expensive purchase you will ever make, so magnitude is important in this case. Here is a solid checklist to get you started on your process:

- Start researching homes as soon as you can. Zillow, Realtor.com, and Trulia are popular options for both buyers and sellers. Once you determine your intended area, you can further narrow your scope by filtering according to price, home type, and other characteristics.
- Determine how much house you can afford. Similar to the process of buying a car, buying a house involves calculating a maximum purchase price. According to Discover, "lenders generally recommend that people look for homes that cost no more than three to five times their annual household income if the home buyers plan to make a 20% down payment and have a moderate amount of other debt." By way of example, a couple earning $100,000 per year on a gross basis should assume a purchase price upper limit of $300,000 to $500,000.
- Try to get prequalified for your mortgage. You don't need to wait until you've found a house to start the

loan qualification process. Before you get deeper into the process, you can provide your mortgage banker with basic financial information such as income and savings figures. The banker will take this information and determine how much they can lend you. This determination will give you some insight into the price range of the homes you can afford. Also, this step will save you time later on when it's time to close on a property. You wouldn't want to miss out on a great deal because of paperwork delays.
- Find the right real estate agent. These individuals can give you first-hand knowledge of homes and neighborhoods, which will help you make an educated decision. The sellers generally pay agents, so you shouldn't have to worry about any charges incurred for these services. Nevertheless, be sure to understand that agents often work in the best interest of their client (the seller, not the buyer).
- Get a home inspection. An inspection will protect you from any unforeseen issues with the house. Your agent will help you set up the review as part of the deal.
- Choose your loan with the help of a mortgage banker. They will spell out your options, and you will go from there.
- Allow the lender to hire a third party to appraise the property. An appraisal will give everyone clarity on the fairness of the agreed-upon purchase price.
- Coordinate the paperwork and close the sale. Your lender will make sure the seller is the rightful owner of the house, and you will subsequently sign all necessary paperwork.

Once you send the check to the seller, congratulations are in order! You've completed the entire home-buying process relatively unscathed! Many people consider the process to be both exciting and painstaking at the same time. On the one hand, you're incredibly excited when you find one or more places where you see yourself fitting. On the other hand, expecting to complete the above steps in less than two months is likely unrealistic. Clearly, there is much work needed to get from start to finish with buying houses. It would be nice if we could purchase houses similar to how we buy cars, where you can sometimes complete the transaction from start to finish in a single day. Unfortunately, this doesn't leave nearly enough room for the moving parts involved, so we'll have to make due until further technological advances come along to create efficiencies within the process.

I mentioned the bit about prequalifying for a mortgage within the above list. The work done during this step will greatly help you narrow down your potential monthly payment. Once you have an upper and lower bound (which should come from the offer given by your mortgage banker), you can insert a line item into your budget. To stay conservative in practice, I would advise that you anchor your expectations to a number closer to the upper bound. You will be mentally prepared to deal with the larger figure. If your actual monthly payment ends up materially lower, you will have extra savings to put to work. We discussed this idea of conservatism when we touched on budgeting, so I'm sure it's no surprise that we'd want to hope for the best but prepare for the worst.

As we've seen, there are several financial aspects to consider when going through this process. For most people, saving up for a down payment seems to be the most challenging part. A 20% down payment on a $300,000 home would total $60,000, plus origination fees associated with the mortgage. You would reach this goal if you saved $985 per month over five years, provided that you used a High Yield Savings Account, or HYSA (these accounts currently yield about 0.60% as of November of 2020). Alternatively, if you happened to start with $10,000, your required savings decreases to about $816 per month. The table on the next page shows these results in visual format.

House Purchase of $300,000 (0.60% Interest Rate on Savings, Down Payment of 20%)			
Starting Capital	Down Payment ($)	Months to Save	Required Savings per Month
$0	$60,000	60	$985.32
$10,000	$60,000	60	$816.10

There are a few investment options that are suitable for this time frame. However, I must admit that being all-in on stocks with your down payment is generally not the best idea. You can use Certificates of Deposit (CDs), which are very similar to savings accounts but pay a fixed rate for a set amount of time. You can often find CDs paying a higher rate than an HYSA for durations longer than one year. These instruments usually pay more interest for longer durations, similar to bonds. If you're looking to take more risk, you can buy ETFs or mutual funds that track bond indices. These will not have as much downside risk as stocks, but you won't participate in as much upside either. Some ideas here include BND, VGSH, and VGLT. BND invests in many different types of bonds, VGSH is strictly short-term Treasuries, and VGLT is strictly long-term Treasuries. All three are ETFs issued by Vanguard, one of the biggest companies heavily involved in the passive management space. I've personally used Vanguard for my retirement funds, and I can speak highly of both their investment options and their customer service.

As much as I love stocks as an avenue to wealth generation, I don't believe they are well-suited for down payment savings. This statement is especially true for periods shorter than 5 to 7 years. Even if we think the market will turn a particular direction, there are no guarantees. Additionally, the risk of substantial drawdowns in short time frames is too significant to risk anything more than a small portion of your savings. If your goal is to accumulate $50,000, and you want to risk $5,000 in stocks, you have some upside potential without risking a large portion of your funds. As with much of this text, there is no one single answer for everyone. The strategy you choose to implement will depend on your risk tolerance and how well you can stomach volatility. It is unfortunate for savers that rates are so low, but you'll have to reconcile this fact with the counterpoint that only bank deposits, CDs, and U.S. Treasuries can be considered risk-free. If you're going to go with stocks regardless, I would first start with companies that pay dividends. Shares of those companies are often perceived as more stable because the companies are more mature than the average company. Also, the price of dividend-paying stocks isn't generally dependent on the revenue growth rate. Once you start investing, you'll see that dividends often act as a buffer for stocks. Stocks that do not pay dividends are more volatile than their dividend-paying counterparts.

One crucial aspect of mortgages to consider is that lenders will look at your current debt payments for insight into your ability to pay. They will compare your current monthly obligations to your monthly income and base your loan amount on this relationship. Lenders often prefer to see a debt-to-income ratio (DTI) of less than 36% (I'm not sure why this is such an exact number). This figure is part of a broader rule called the "28/36 Rule," which states that "a household should spend a maximum of 28% of its gross monthly income on total housing expenses; it should spend no more than 36% on total debt service, including housing and other debt such as car loans." This rule simply means that individuals with heightened debt obligations will have less capacity to borrow money for a mortgage.

In contrast, those who have more disposable income will have higher borrowing limits. If you happen to have student loans, car loans, or both, I advise that you calculate your DTI before you head to the bank. Taking a few minutes to do this will help you see where you stand, and you'll be more prepared to answer questions from the mortgage banker when you do go to prequalify. There are calculators available online that will perform this math for you. I have included one example for you in the References section at the back of this book.

We went through much material in this chapter regarding debt. I hope that this chat gave you further background on the inner workings of credit cards, auto loans, and mortgages. Here are the key takeaways that can help us going forward:

Credit Cards

- Monthly line of credit that comes with a high interest rate.
- Many cards include cash, mile, or statement credit rewards to encourage spending.
- Late payments can damage your credit history, which will make obtaining future loans terms less favorable for you. Conversely, paying on time will often increase credit scores over time.
- Credit cards offer flexibility for budgeting and occasionally contain a 0% interest clause for an introductory period.

Auto Loans

- Car loans often span 3 to 6 years in duration, though this can vary depending on your needs and approval from the lender.
- Interest rates here are comparable to mortgage interest rates, between 5% to 10% at the current moment. They are dependent on creditworthiness.
- There is often no down payment requirement for car loans. However, if you're able to pull together a 20% payment, this will help reduce your loan payments (and, by association, your interest costs).
- Using online calculators can help you determine your personal maximum purchase price. This price can change based on your inputs of loan duration, interest rates, and maximum monthly loan payment.
- Your insurance payment may change based on the car you purchase and on the number of vehicles insured. Older cars generally come with lower insurance payments than their newer counterparts.

Mortgages

- We outlined an 8-step process that will take you from the research stage through the closing phase.
- Saving for a down payment, especially while living in a high cost-of-living area, can be the most challenging part of the process. We considered investment options such as HYSAs, CDs, and bond ETFs. You can explore stocks if you are putting a small percentage of your funds in the market. Having more time to stomach volatility also helps the argument for stocks.
- Your Debt-to-Income (DTI) is essential to calculate and understand because lenders will use this number when determining your maximum borrowing capacity. The rule-of-thumb is 28/36, where we aim to keep our housing expenses below 28% of income and total debt payments below 36% of income.
- As with auto loans, our budgeting goal is to arrive at a monthly payment less than the maximum allowable based on our circumstances. As an example, if we can comfortably afford a $1,000 payment, we will want to pay no more than $900 per month. This practice provides a modest 10% buffer where we can reinvest the difference between our maximum allocation and our payment.

With our discussion on debt finally completed, I want to thank you for being open to learning about the most prevalent types of consumer debt. Liabilities and expenses are often burdensome for people to discuss because of their nature. Still, this information is invaluable and will help you both now and in the future. I want you to take advantage of all options at your disposal. To this end, I'm glad you've decided to take this step and further your education of credit cards, auto loans, and mortgages. Those of you with student loans will need to pay special attention to the previous chapter and combine this knowledge with your understanding of traditional consumer debts.

      The next chapter will focus on wedding and marriage planning. The financial implications of this important life event are far-reaching in many respects, so it's worthwhile to examine best practices. We all want to start our lives with our special someone with a solid foundation in place. To achieve this, we can dedicate some time here to think deeply about our present and future relationship from an economic context.

Chapter 6: Wedding and Marriage Planning

Weddings often represent one of the most memorable times in our lives. You are setting out to wed the person you want to be with for the rest of your days. Forgetting about finances for a second, this is a big day! As much as personal finance sometimes has a rational and mathematically correct choice, emotions are what drive personal relationships. It also doesn't come with the same sort of strategizing handbook. Simply put, only you will know whether this decision is the right one. The advice contained herein might not be as relevant to those of you uninterested in marriage. Even so, this knowledge could come in handy if you decide to change your mind in the future or if you are in a relationship that doesn't involve marriage. Becoming further experienced with financial planning, creating budgets, and getting on the same page will always be in style. With that said, let's dive into critical points we'll want to keep in mind when going through this stage of life.

The cost of having a wedding has increased materially in recent years. According to NerdWallet, the average cost of a wedding in 2019 was $33,900. This figure includes the engagement ring, ceremony, and reception. The most expensive part of any wedding is often the venue, with an average cost of over $15,000 in 2019. You and your partner might have different views on weddings. Some people are looking for big weddings with plenty of people, while others would prefer a smaller event. Once you both agree that this is what you want, try to determine a fair cost or a range of expenses that won't break the bank. All things equal, we would prefer to refrain from taking on debt to finance a wedding. The idea is that you should be able to afford the big day between personal savings and any gifts from both sides of the family.

Saving for a wedding is often a multi-year process. Most people don't have $35,000 to shell out on a whim, especially those in the first few years of their careers. This idea is doubly true for those carrying student loans. However, all hope is not lost. If you're able to save $350 per month, it will take you eight years to reach the average cost figure stated in the above paragraph. Continuing this idea, if your partner is also able to save $350 per month, the time needed to reach $33,900 will be cut in half. Finally, an increase to a total savings of $1,000 per month will cut down the time to just under three years, a far cry from our original suggestion of eight years.

Each family will have a distinct financial situation. Some families might be able to give, while others will have constraints that do not allow them to help. For this reason, creating a blueprint for a wedding budget is nearly impossible. It doesn't help that many individuals have trouble talking about money with close family members. To stay conservative, you can assume that you and your partner will pay for all expenses and that your families won't be able to help at all. While we often see families assisting the couple in paying for wedding expenses, advising anything other than conservatism in our estimates would contradict the rest of this text.

Each family will take to these approaches differently. Some prefer more direct communication, while others would prefer a softer conversation. It will be up to you to determine what is best for your family. This part shouldn't be too difficult as you likely know their preferred mode of communication.

I want to make it clear that paying for a wedding is stressful. That said, please know that parents often want to help their children. Involving your families in the conversation will increase transparency and allow them to voice how they feel about the wedding finances. At the outset, wedding planning is daunting and induces anxiety for many people. Involving your parents will help you take a deep breath and gain clarity on their feelings.

However, not everyone has a nuclear family. Some of you might not be able to have your family involved because of strained relationships. Others lost family members at a young age. For those of you who fall into any of these categories, don't lose hope. When planning your wedding, you may consider leaning on trusted friends or members of your extended family with whom you have a good relationship. You'll need to tap into your network of trusted individuals who can help you manage all of the moving parts. You might feel alone at times, but this is your opportunity to create stronger bonds among those who are special to you. You can do this!

In certain situations, both sides of a couple will find it appropriate to create and sign a prenuptial agreement (also known as a prenup). This agreement can help define the legal rights of both people and helps determine what happens upon death or divorce. The vast majority of couples do not enter into a prenup. However, these agreements have recently become more common. Prenups are gaining popularity with millennials for two reasons: "Americans are getting married later, accumulating more assets and debt before marriage, and many millennials are children of divorce, making them predisposed to protect their interests." The American Academy of Matrimonial Lawyers conducted a survey and reported that "more than half of lawyers surveyed saw an increase in prenups among millennials, and 62% saw a rise in prenups overall from 2013 to 2016." Depending on your situation, you might find it useful to talk to your partner about whether this is appropriate for you. The common theme with this chapter will be that you need to be in lockstep with your partner as much as possible, and this same logic should apply to prenups. Prenups can reduce stress incurred during divorce because there is less uncertainty regarding the outcome of asset distribution and other related financial matters. From taking this point of view, I can see why some couples find them useful. As always, inquire about your partner's thoughts and take it from there.

Keeping with the theme of communication, I want to stress the importance of chatting with your spouse about your financial past, present, and future. Assets, liabilities, and income don't seem to be fun points of discussion for most. Even so, it's imperative that you understand each other's previous decisions, current situation, goals, and dreams. This conversation will help you build trust and is a wonderful starting point from which you can plan your future together. It's likely that you already have a sense of their current picture and where they see themselves going, so you might have already put this principle into practice. Transparency and openness in this stage of your life will make planning for the future more streamlined and will create a stronger bond between the two of you. Though this chapter attempts to help you and your partner prepare financially, this section also recognizes the importance of strengthening your overall relationship. As an example, I've seen my parents frequently touch base on financial matters just to keep transparency prioritized and confirm that everyone has adequate information. Involving your spouse in decisions big and small will be appreciated and will likely be reciprocated as well.

You and your partner should also determine whether you will be keeping separate accounts or joint accounts. The latter seems to be the more popular option, though there can be good reasons for different accounts. Couples often report feeling a lack of financial independence when using a joint account, so separate accounts could help alleviate this issue. Also, if the marriage ends, joint accounts will cause more difficulties than will separate accounts. There are benefits to using joint accounts as well, and there are several reasons why they are the preferred option for the majority of couples. Perhaps the chief reason for this is the emotional closeness couples feel when using a joint account. In a study of 1,000 married couples, 65% of couples who used joint accounts reported being happier in their relationships. Joint accounts also simplify paying bills and aggregate savings. As a result, it's easier to determine your total assets and liabilities as a couple if you keep funds within one central account. Also, since income and expenses are easier to track within one account, there is less chance of any positive or negative surprises. One example might include your partner earning or spending money without telling you. I can also imagine situations where one partner is the breadwinner by a considerable degree and might have issues with a joint account. Individuals in this predicament might worry that their partner will take advantage of their financial situation. Ultimately, how you and your partner choose to deal with and feel about this situation will be the key to your success. Whichever way you lean, make sure to talk with your partner about what your bank account situation will look like in the future.

In the Budgeting chapter, we discussed different

budgeting tactics and how we can think about planning monthly income and expenses. This same logic can be applied to your relationship as well. Whether you are planning to pay costs separately or jointly, creating a budget with your partner will help you organize the different line items. If you both choose to keep separate financial lives, you can each create a distinct budget tailored to your income and itemized expenses. Either way, it's a good idea to list out all debts as separate line items. As modern management thinker Peter Drucker has stated, "If you can't measure it, you can't improve it."

One last suggestion for wedding and marriage planning involves discussing different types of insurance. You ideally want both individuals to be covered under your medical, dental, and vision plans. If one of you has comparatively better coverage for medical, while the other has the advantage within dental, you can arrange your affairs to maximize value. In this example, you might look to cover your partner with your medical insurance while your partner covers you with their dental plan. Many employer plans allow partners to be covered as long as you both meet certain conditions. Some require a certain amount of cohabitation time before coverage commencing, while others might require marriage altogether. Maximizing utility will both save you money and reduce any anxiety about insurance coverage.

A recap of what we've learned about wedding and marriage planning is as follows:

- The average cost of a wedding in the U.S. is $33,900, but all hope is not lost.
- Not every family will be able to help with wedding expenses. If this is the case for you, or if you don't have any family on which to rely, try to lean on trusted friends during this process.
- Some people decide to sign a prenuptial agreement. Regardless of your personal leanings, confirming your plan with your partner is the best way forward.
- Be sure to talk with your partner about debts, financial goals for the future, and whether you plan to keep separate accounts or use a joint account

- instead. Based on the choice of account organization, create the appropriate number of budgets to reflect your finances accurately.
- Make sure to maximize value as a couple by discussing insurance coverage and how you can save money efficiently.

The next topic we will tackle will be college planning, not for yourself, but your children. Folks who decide to refrain from having kids might not think they'll need to learn about college planning. Still, I believe everyone must obtain at least a basic understanding of how to plan for significant expenses occurring years into the future. Let's do it!

Chapter 7: Planning College for Your Children

Going to college has become ubiquitous in this country. It has been regarded as a gateway to a middle-class lifestyle. Unfortunately, this notion has led to extreme increases in the cost of a college degree during recent years. We previously discussed the student loan issue extensively within the Student Loan chapter, so I don't believe hashing that out again is necessary here. Instead, I'd like to delve into how you as a parent (or future parent/guardian) can best prepare for this considerable expense. I don't anticipate the 'college push' changing in the foreseeable future, so it might be prudent to stay educated and save yourself and your children from future stress and heartbreak. I am worried that college costs will continue to increase as the 4-year degree further solidifies itself as a barrier to entry into the professional workforce. I am also worried that, if we fail to prepare both ourselves and our children adequately, we will have to make a tough decision. We will be deciding between supporting our children as they take on eye-popping levels of student debt or determining a path that doesn't involve a college degree. For these reasons, we must examine the steps we can take today to alleviate this stress as much as possible.

Every state in the U.S. has options to help you save for a future beneficiary's expenses. These are generally referred to as 529 plans, though each state has its own specific name for the program. 529 plans have significant tax advantages associated with them. These advantages allow your money to grow faster and to reward smart decision-making (as saving money for your beneficiary is a great decision indeed). For example, if you live in New York and decide to contribute to the New York 529 Direct Plan, you will pay no income tax on earnings, and you will be able to make tax-free withdrawals in the future to pay for college expenses. Also, you can get a state income tax deduction when you file your taxes for the year in which you contribute. Again, every state will have a different plan, so do your research in advance before opening an account. Most (if not all) states will allow you to use their program, even if you aren't a resident of that state. It's probably best to stick with the state in which you live, as you'll most likely max out your tax benefit that way.

For those who would like more investment options within their college savings plan, there is another type of account you can consider. The Coverdell Education Savings Account (ESA) is similar to a 529 in that it allows tax-free growth and tax-free withdrawals for qualified education expenses. However, there are two features of Coverdell ESAs that make them worthy of our research. For one, Coverdell ESAs have more expansive investment options than do 529 plans. Within Coverdells, you can invest in individual stocks, real estate, and precious metals with great ease and flexibility. Also, Coverdell plans cover K-12 expenses as well. You can also use the funds for other beneficiaries without much worry, as long as the purpose involves K-12 or college expenses.

To provide a fair picture of these accounts, we should consider the drawbacks as well. One con is that funds within Coverdell accounts must be used before the beneficiary reaches 30 years of age. We can transfer these funds to a 529 plan without much issue, though the age limit is essential to keep in mind. Additionally, there are yearly and income-based contribution limits. No matter your income, the maximum you can contribute per year is $2,000, which doesn't give you much wiggle room. The income limit for Coverdells is $190,000 for this year (2020). This limit makes Coverdells appear less attractive than 529 plans.

Your choice of account will be up to you. However, it's important to note that you can have multiple accounts for a given beneficiary. For most people, I would think that 529s will do the job well. If your state happens to have a lackluster 529 plan, opening a Coverdell ESA could help you meet your goals and give you a valuable fallback option. A chart comparing 529s and Coverdells is attached on the next page for your convenience.

Category	529 Plan	Coverdell ESA
Tax Benefits	Tax-free growth and tax-free withdrawals for qualified education expenses (college).	Tax-free growth and tax-free withdrawals for qualified education expenses (college and K-12).
Investment Options	Fixed portfolios	Individual stocks, funds, real estate, and others
Income Limits and Maximum Contributions	No income limits and no cap on contributions	Income phase-out at $190,000 for joint filers and contribution cap of $2,000

In terms of the investment choices in 529s, most states will give you a fixed list of portfolios from which you can choose. Plans will range from aggressive to conservative, with a balanced option situated in the middle of the risk spectrum. Aggressive plans will be tilted towards stocks, while conservative plans will incline towards bonds. The balanced option will seek to provide lower volatility than a stock-heavy portfolio by allocating funds equally to both stocks and bonds. You should consider starting with the more aggressive options early on, especially if you have more than ten years until your beneficiary will need the money. As time goes on, you should consider switching to more balanced plan options. Your expected annual return should decrease over the years, but your risk will decrease as well. Some companies, such as Vanguard, also have age-based options where the plan will automatically shift the highest risk towards the early years. These portfolios allocate more funds to bonds and less to stocks over time. For example, the conservative option at Vanguard starts as a 60% stock/40% bond portfolio. After two years, this allocation changes to 50% stock and 50% bonds. This shift continues until your child is 18 and ready to attend college, at which point the allocation will shift to either all-cash or a mix of bonds and cash. Your choice of portfolio will be a product of your risk appetite. Gaining experience in the realm of investing can help you determine your comfortability with volatility. It would be beneficial to have this experience before choosing between these allocations, though I wouldn't say it's necessary. Nevertheless, you should research the different 529 investment managers, their plans, and how you can leverage these options to create a valuable difference in your child's future education.

One of the principal determinants of college planning success is your continued contribution schedule. If you can find a way to contribute monthly, that would greatly help you achieve your goals. Even $100 per month can add up over time, especially within the context of an 18-year investment horizon. As an example, we can assume that when our child is born, we start with a principal value of $10,000 invested in a growth-oriented 529 plan. If we contribute $100 per month, and if the plan grows at an average rate of 8% per year, the final value of the plan would total $90,014.35. At current prices, this sum would pay for a student to attend a state school for four years and would cover tuition as well as room and board. If we bump up our contribution amount to $150 per month and keep all other inputs the same, the final value would equal $114,018.66. It is essential to consider that inflation will eat into this value going forward. We cannot expect college prices to stay at current levels indefinitely, so we need to account for this by increasing contributions where we can. If you have a one-time bonus you can spare, this can help accelerate gains over the long term.

With compounding, the longer your money is allowed to grow, the better your results will be. Most young couples are not able to front-load their 529 contributions. This statement is often true because couples who are just having children now are still relatively early in their careers. They also don't have excess capital available to tie up in investments. However, it is in your best interest to find a way to put some money away early, to the extent that this is possible. If we run the same example as before (with inputs of 8% annual growth, $100 per month contribution, and $10,000 starting balance), we obtain a result of $90,000 at the end of 18 years. If we change the starting balance to $30,000 and keep all other inputs the same, we obtain a result of about $150,000. From this point, we can even cut our monthly contribution down to nothing and still finish with about $126,000, $36,000 more than the first example. The difference in final value underscores the idea that front-loading can help you create wealth over the long term. You might not have a large sum available to invest when your child is born. Even so, the best thing you can do for yourself is to set a monthly contribution schedule and stay persistent. Your diligence will reap the rewards over the long-term. As a final example, monthly contributions of $400 for the 18 years (at 8% growth) would lead to a final value of $192,034.45! I urge you to play around with investment calculators and see how the final values change based on your inputs. You'll likely be surprised at the magnitude to which contribution schedule and investment horizon have on future growth and final portfolio value.

If the annual increase in college costs over the last ten years persists for the next ten years, we're in for a rude awakening. According to Vanguard, college costs have been increasing by an annual rate of 5% for some time. If this rate persists, a degree could cost 62% more in 10 years and 140% more (more than double!) in 18 years. With this in mind, you shouldn't focus on saving the entire amount of future gross costs. Instead, we can aim to end with about a third of the cost covered. The logic here is that scholarships, financial aid, and future income can round out the rest of the pie. We want to balance your goals for yourself with your goal of reducing your child's debt coming out of school, and this mindset is an excellent way to achieve this goal.

Now we know that our objective is to save for a third of net college expenses. What sort of contribution schedule will accomplish this task? For practicality's sake, a strategy centered on monthly contributions will probably work best. This way, it's not so frequent that it becomes a bother but not infrequent enough that it becomes difficult to budget. Also, most people like to budget monthly, so we should have no issues adding monthly contributions as a potential line item. For most plans, you can set a custom schedule. Perhaps the most crucial part is that you practice consistency and diligence with your contributions. Staying the course will prove immensely valuable, not only throughout your investing career but also in life generally. The best time to invest is often when volatility is rampant and people are scared of losing money because of recent market plunges. Over long periods, every previous market downdraft has proven to be an excellent time to put capital to work. This statement is true, at minimum, when looking at broad-based index funds. It's also true that long-term investors who bought at market tops have still been rewarded handsomely, so you don't necessarily need to pick bottoms here. The key is to execute our strategy. If our strategy is solid, we know that staying the course is the right decision.

Some colleges are more expensive to attend, while others come with more modest rates. Namely, NYU's cost of attendance totals approximately $78,000 for on-campus students. In contrast, Stony Brook University (my alma mater) boasts a cost of about $28,000 for an in-state on-campus student. That's a difference of $50,000 per year or $200,000 over the life of a 4-year degree. If you were to take the difference between these two costs and invest that over 44 years (4 years for the degree and 40 years after that), we would obtain a final value at age 62 of $4,894,656.35. In the previous calculation, we assume an 8% annual return and no further contributions besides the $50,000 over the first four years. This exercise demonstrates both the power of compounding and the implicit decision made when choosing a higher-priced school. In this case, you've determined that the experience gained through this particular school is worth the extra cost. You can think of this from a purely financial perspective, where you believe your child will have the best chance of success by matriculating in a given school. You would be betting that the potential for your child's future salary is so significant from attending this school that you will invest in your child's education. This action would be at the expense of putting those funds into the market or otherwise driving asset growth over time.

Conversely, you can also think of this from a more emotional perspective. You want to see your child happy, and you notice that they fit in a particular setting that happens to have a higher cost. Choosing a college is not solely a business transaction, so please don't think I'm trying to suck the feelings and emotions that naturally come with such a big decision. I'm merely attempting to shed light on this topic by presenting a different viewpoint. The opportunity cost is higher when we think about making potential investments than if we think about merely keeping the funds in cash. I do want to highlight that the above example with $200,000 invested over four years might not apply to everyone because it would be difficult to obtain a loan for that amount of funds. It would also be impossible to get a personal loan for investments with an interest rate comparable to that associated with student loans (8%-10% vs. 4%-7%). Practicality notwithstanding, I do believe the example has merit and that it underscores the essence of the college decision from a financial standpoint.

Getting back to setting a contribution schedule, I do think monthly deposits will often be the best fit for most people. Regardless of our chosen plan, it will be essential to know how much we need to contribute if we want to reach our goals. If we aim to achieve the one-third of the cost goal I mentioned above and we use a 529 savings plan, our estimated monthly contributions will look something like this:

- Public (in-state): $210/month
- Public (out-of-state): $330/month
- Private: $415/month

Given these estimates, we can see that the projected contribution amount does depend on the choice of school. Of course, there will be many years where you are uncertain regarding your child's choice of school. You really can't get a good grasp of this before they start high school, which is 14 years into the 18-year journey of saving for college. Since there will be uncertainty for some time, you can try to start your contributions within the middle of this range and scale up or down when you have more information available. At a contribution of $330 per month and a growth assumption of 8% per year, the final value upon matriculation would be $158,000. If you don't yet have the means to contribute $330 per month, you can consider finding the midpoint between the two public school options listed above. A contribution of $250 per month could potentially lead to a final value of $120,000, which should be enough to put a sizable dent in your child's college bill. Just as no one can predict the future growth of your investments, no one can predict the future growth of college costs. Even so, we'll try to stay within our means, contribute monthly, and grow our funds to help support our children.

I happen to know several recent graduates who took loans to pay for school. Someone just coming into their own as an adult will have a hard time accumulating any funds to pay for tuition, room and board, and other fees. Of course, all families have a right to deal with this issue however they want. Some parents aren't in a position to help, while still others would prefer that their now-adult child handles it themselves. In my writings within this chapter, I don't mean to imply that all parents should feel responsible for this financial burden. Parents also need not feel regret if they don't have the means to help. The purpose of this chapter is to shed light on the available college planning options in case you were not previously aware of their existence. Whether you will take this and incorporate it into your own life will be up to you. If we can put a reasonable amount away each month, let this money grow, and help relieve our children of future stress, I think we should try to do this. Readers under 30 are likely still dealing with their own student loan issues. They are not ready to turn the focus over to something that might or might not happen in the future. For those of you in this category, the information contained in this chapter will be available to you whenever that time comes. I hope that these tips make tackling this issue just a little bit easier.

Most of you will likely choose to use 529 plans to save on behalf of your beneficiary, as they are the most popular choice for this purpose. It would make sense for us to examine the potential tax benefits and other related changes this will make to your tax situation. Blanket generalizations aren't possible here because each state administers a separate and distinct 529 plan targeted to its constituents. However, we can still become familiar with the tax benefits common to many 529 plans.

First, there are two types of 529 plans: education savings plans and prepaid tuition plans. Our discussion so far has revolved around education savings plans, which allow savers to open an investment account and invest accordingly. As a result of the 2017 Tax Cuts and Jobs Act, savers can now use 529 plans to pay up to $10,000 per child per year for any K-12 tuition. This addendum seems to make Coverdells less attractive because the main draw of Coverdells was the ability to use funds for K-12 education as well as college costs.

While education savings plans allow for direct investments in mutual funds and ETFs, prepaid tuition plans allow savers to purchase credits at participating colleges and universities. The main draw for this plan is that you are buying future credits for your child at current tuition rates. This plan generally does not allow payments towards future room and board. Also, these plans do not allow payments towards tuition for elementary and secondary schools. These two attributes make the prepaid plan less flexible than the education savings plan. There is one chief risk with prepaid plans worth mentioning. If your child doesn't attend a participating college or university, the plan might pay less than its original intention. In essence, if your child decides to attend a school that isn't covered by the program, you might be penalized. Since you are getting discounted credits for participating in the plan, it makes sense that only particular schools would participate themselves. Perhaps the best benefit of prepaid plans is the security that they offer. Savers need not worry about market fluctuations or balancing risk and return. They are virtually guaranteed to earn a return on their investment, so long as their child decides to attend one of the participating schools. If it doesn't pan out that way, these plans could fail to give you the expected return on investment. Locking your child's future into a particular college or set of colleges might be difficult. Still, it could be worth your while if you want the security inherent in this program.

With this new grasp of the two main types of 529 plans, we can investigate the valuable tax benefits. First, the bad: 529 contributions are not tax-deductible on the federal level. 529s have a different setup than 401(k) plans, where contributions are shielded from current-day taxable income and are taxed later. We will discuss 401(k)s extensively in the "Planning for Retirement" chapter. Another drawback is the 10% penalty and applicable tax on all non-qualified withdrawals of investment gains. Like you will soon see with 401(k)s, 529 plans punish those who don't follow the rules and either take money out too early or use funds for a non-qualified reason. As such, we should plan to have this money act as our absolute last resort, available only after we exhaust all other options. By contrast, investing in a brokerage account provides greater flexibility and allows funds to be withdrawn and used for any purpose. However, we'll soon learn why the flexibility of brokerage accounts pale in comparison to the incentives offered by 529 plans.

Now it's time to turn towards the positives! A relevant list of the tax and ownership incentives of 529 plans is as follows:

- Your 529 plan will grow federal tax-free, and you won't be taxed when you eventually take the money out to pay for college. This feature goes for all 529 plans, regardless of the state you pick!
- The government added both student loans and apprenticeship programs as a qualified education expense in 2019, so 529 funds can now be used here with no penalties or taxes levied.
- As of 2020, 34 states offer a full or partial tax deduction for 529 plan contributions. Some of the more prominent states offering full tax deductions include New York, Connecticut, and Illinois. For New York's plan in particular, a couple filing under "Married Filing Jointly" can deduct up to $10,000 from their state taxable income. This deduction can be of great value to a saver: at a 20% tax rate, the maximum tax savings is $2,000 per year, which is not a nominal amount by any means. If your state doesn't offer a deduction, you can choose any other state's plan as well, so please don't feel locked in if your state doesn't have a great offering available.
- As the donor and owner of the account, you stay in control indefinitely. Ownership will never transfer to the beneficiary, so it will be up to you to withdraw the funds when the time comes to use them. With this

setup, it won't be possible for the beneficiary to spend the funds wastefully because you will retain ownership through the account's life.
- Tax reporting is simple with 529 plans. You don't need to report 529 contributions on any tax forms, and you will only receive a 1099 form in the year in which you withdraw the funds.

After all of this discussion mainly centered on 529 plans, you might be wondering why we don't just use a standard brokerage account to save and invest for college. There are three reasons for this, which I will spell out on the next page:

- Most notably, taxable brokerage accounts fail to offer the tax incentives offered by 529 plans. Gains will be taxed at a minimum of 15% (the current long-term capital gains tax rate) and could be taxed north of 30% based on your portfolio turnover and level of income. Also, no states offer deductions for brokerage account contributions. Therefore, we are missing two critical benefits here if we decide to use a taxable brokerage account.
- While some of you might be interested in creating your own portfolio, there is a chance that this portfolio will underperform one that is created by a professional as part of the 529 plan.
- If funds designated for college are in a brokerage account, there's nothing to stop you from withdrawing the money and using it for other purposes. In a way, the 10% penalty involved with early 529 withdrawals acts as a deterrent to this behavior. Thankfully, most people adhere to this rule and stay on track to hit their goals. You can think of the penalty as a disincentive for early withdrawal. In my view, we should not take this lightly.

For these reasons, I strongly advise that you consider using 529 plans over brokerage accounts for future college savings. The tax incentives are hard to beat, and there is great value in investing passively and letting your consistency dictate your results over time.

The benefits of 529s are clear at this point. In my view, using a 529 plan is the best way to save for a future college expense. The prepaid tuition plan is a decent idea. However, it doesn't give the family enough optionality to change their minds regarding the choice of school later on in the process. 529s have the tax incentives, investment options, and overall structure to help you succeed in saving for college, no matter where your child decides to attend school.

Now that our discussion on college planning has ended, we can recap it as follows:

- There are two distinct routes for those looking to save for college: 529 plans and Coverdell Education Savings Accounts.
- We can split 529 plans into two further plans: prepaid tuition plans, which allow savers to purchase future credits at current prices, and education savings plans, which enable savers to invest funds in various portfolios and later use the funds for qualified education expenses.
- For education savings plans (my preferred choice for savers), consistent monthly contributions can help us save money over time. One example we looked at involved monthly contributions of $400 for 18 years. With growth of 8% per year, we arrived at a final value of just over $192,000, which can give you wonderful optionality when college time comes around.
- Our goal is not to save for the full cost of college, but instead to cover one-third of the net price by making consistent investments over a long period. I don't want to belabor the point, but we need to remember that compound interest is our friend! Starting as early as possible can help you more than you might have realized when you started reading this book.
- If you can, try to make a separate line item for your

monthly contribution, and please do your best to stick to it! If applicable, please be sure to deduct the maximum possible amount from your state taxable income.
- In my opinion, using a 529 education savings plan is the best way to save for college due to their mix of investment options, choice of college flexibility, and incredibly generous tax incentives.

In the next chapter, we'll cover how to save for retirement. We will also see why it is, yet again, imperative to start saving as early as possible.

Chapter 8: Planning for Retirement

The ultimate financial goal for most people is to retire from work and enjoy the rest of their days as they wish. Unfortunately, many Americans aren't well-prepared for retirement, often relying on family members and government assistance to merely survive after working for multiple decades. We can attribute much of this to rising healthcare costs, inadequate saving practices during career years, and the increases in lifespan due to better medicine and technology. In this chapter, I will explain how we can better prepare ourselves financially to make sure we enjoy the "golden years."

Previously, many companies offered pension plans to their employees. Within this structure, both employers and employees would set aside money in a pot, which would grow indefinitely. When employees retired, they would be able to collect paychecks from the pot in a regular fashion. Some employers still do this, but within the last few decades, many employers have switched to offering 401(k) plans. In 1978, a section was added to the Internal Revenue Code that permits employers to provide retirement plans to their employees. These plans invest employee money in the market on a pre-tax basis. You effectively defer your taxes until you take the money out during retirement. This setup allows for your money to grow without being taxed first. You also save on today's tax bill, which is a nice benefit as well. Additionally, as many as 75% of companies will match at least part of your 401(k) contribution.

To illustrate, suppose our employer matches 50% of our contribution, up to 6% of our paycheck. If we contribute 6% of every paycheck to our 401(k), our employer will provide 3% as well, for a total of 9%. You've virtually guaranteed yourself a 50% return right off the bat, due to the employer match. That's not even counting investment gains! When you look at the matching from that perspective, it's easy to see why everyone should be putting in as much as they can spare, up to the maximum match (if applicable). An example scenario has been attached on the next page.

Contribution Table for Employee Earning $50,000			
Employee Contribution (6%)	Employer Contribution (3%)	Total Contribution ($)	Total Contribution (%)
$3,000.00	$1,500.00	$4,500.00	9.00%

401(k) plans have some rules, restrictions, and limits, so it would be best to highlight them now before we go any further. To contribute to a 401(k), your employer must sponsor a plan. If you are self-employed, you can start your own Solo 401(k), which comes with slightly different rules and limits. Otherwise, you'll be encountering the standard 401(k) plan, which will be detailed here. As of the 2019-2020 tax year, you can contribute up to $19,500, and an extra $6,500 if you are 50 or older. This additional stipulation is called the 'catch-up contribution,' where older workers can contribute more as they are approaching retirement age.

401(k) plans also have something called required minimum distributions (RMDs). Starting at age 72, you are required to withdraw a certain amount from your 401(k). This amount depends on your account balance as well as your life expectancy, so there is no clear-cut percentage or dollar amount to calculate. However, there are calculators you can find with a simple web search that will estimate your RMD, given those factors. RMDs are not desirable for savers, as anytime you withdraw from your investment account, you lessen your account's potential for gains. This point is something to consider if you plan on contributing to a 401(k). However, I don't believe this should deter anyone from participating in one during their career. In 401(k) plans, you can only invest in funds that your employer offers. For example, if your company only offers mutual funds or index funds from one broker, you don't have much choice in the matter. 401(k) plans generally don't allow investment in individual stocks, so if you are looking to invest in those, there is another type of account called an IRA. We will touch on this account after our discussion of 401(k) plans has concluded. Another option, depending on if your employer offers it, is a Roth 401(k). This account is slightly different from the traditional 401(k) in that the money allocated for the plan is taxed before investment takes place. As a result, you don't save on today's tax bill by using this plan. However, when you take the money out during your retirement years, you won't have to pay any taxes on it. Whatever balance you have in your account, you will know that all of it is rightly yours, with no other person or entity having any claim to it. These plans are not offered by most employers, as many stick to the traditional 401(k). If you're someone who would rather pay the relevant taxes now to earn tax-free withdrawals later, a Roth 401(k) could be a great fit. If you don't happen to know what your employer offers, HR will likely be more than happy to discuss your employer-sponsored options.

At this point, it would be prudent to discuss your individual retirement options, which are not dependent on the characteristics of your employer. The most popular route is the Individual Retirement Account, or IRA. This account is a tax-advantaged account designed to help you save for retirement. In this case, you would be opening one as an individual (no employer needs to sponsor you). The maximum yearly contribution to these accounts is lower than that of the 401(k). For example, in the 2020 tax year, you can contribute up to $6,000 on an annual basis (versus $19,500 for the 401(k)). These limits are increased every few years by the IRS, so it's a good idea to stay informed about them.

Just like the employer-sponsored plans we previously discussed, we can split IRAs into two types, Traditional and Roth. In using a Traditional IRA, you get to defer your taxes until you use the funds in your retirement years. This deferral results in a nice tax break for the year in which you contribute. The rules for taking the deduction are not that simple, and it's imperative to know the particulars and stipulations of these things before jumping in. Depending on your income level and whether or not you participate in an employer-sponsored retirement plan, your maximum deduction might vary. As with contributions to a Roth 401(k), contributions to a Roth IRA are not tax-deductible. However, the advantage of a Roth IRA is that, since the IRS has already taxed your funds, you won't be taxed when you take the money out in retirement. The appeal here is that neither your contributions nor your gains will be subject to taxes at the onset of your retirement. I know the Roth IRA works best for me because I much prefer to pay taxes now to earn tax-free withdrawals later on. Like much of this text, your choice here will be a personal one. A good thing to consider is that you can have both a Traditional IRA and a Roth IRA. If you choose to keep both types of accounts, you'll just need to make sure that your annual contributions to both of these accounts sum up to less than the annual contribution limit.

    The second benefit of an IRA is that you have a bevy of investment vehicles from which to choose. In contrast, in a 401(k), you are limited to the options your employer provides. Brokers such as Vanguard, Fidelity, and TD Ameritrade offer both types of accounts. In choosing a broker, there are a few things to consider. The most important considerations, in my estimation, are cost structure and investment options. Make sure to choose a broker that will fit your needs, whatever is important to you. Opening an account with them should be reasonably straightforward and shouldn't require more than 15 minutes of your time. Starting to save for retirement is one of the best financial and life decisions you can make, and I implore you to spend some time creating an account. Also, you generally don't have to fund the account when you create it. I hope that every American adult eventually opens and uses an IRA, whether Traditional or Roth, to take control of their retirement. To make the comparison more manageable, I've attached a chart on the next page for your convenience.

Types of Retirement Accounts				
Category	Roth 401(k)	401(k)	Roth IRA	IRA
Tax Benefits	Withdrawals of your contributions and growth is tax-free, while withdrawals of your employer's contributions and growth will be taxable within retirement.	Withdrawals of your contributions and growth will be taxed, but you will get an income deduction in the current year.	Withdrawals of your contributions and growth will be tax-free, but you will not get an income deduction in the current year.	Withdrawals of your contributions and growth will be taxed, but you will get an income deduction in the current year.
Investment Options	Fixed portfolios	Fixed portfolios	Individual stocks, funds, real estate, and others	Individual stocks, funds, real estate, and others
Income Limits and Maximum Contributions	Up to $19,500 with a $6,000 catch-up for those 50 or older. No income limit.	Up to $19,500 with a $6,000 catch-up for those 50 or older. No income limit.	Up to $6,000 with a $1,000 catch-up for those 50 or older. Income phases-out at $124,000 for single filers and $196,000 for joint filers.	Up to $6,000 with a $1,000 catch-up for those 50 or older. Income phases-out at $124,000 for single filers and $196,000 for joint filers (you can contribute but no deduction will be granted).
Account Type	Employer-Sponsored	Employer-Sponsored	Personal Account	Personal Account
RMD	Yes, after 72 years of age	Yes, after 72 years of age	No	Yes, after 72 years of age

An important fact to note is that you need to be at least 59 ½ years of age to withdraw money from any of these accounts without penalties. If you withdraw before this point, you will pay a 10% penalty. You'll also pay any relevant deferred taxes as well. Please be sure to keep this in mind because you wouldn't want to make a mistake by not knowing the rules for retirement account withdrawals.

Once we have an account, we then need to fund the account and choose how we are going to invest the funds. Traditional investments in IRAs include stocks, bonds, mutual funds, and ETFs. The sheer number of options might be overwhelming at first. We went over the alternatives in a previous chapter, so I won't go into detail here. Asset allocation, how you organize your investments, is going to vary based mostly on your risk tolerance, age, and familiarity with the investment vehicles themselves. Those who have a higher risk tolerance will be content using individual stocks in their portfolio. At the same time, more risk-averse investors will shy away from the same, given the lack of easy diversification. Concerning retirement investing, younger investors have more time until they reach retirement age, so that would lead them to have a long time horizon for investment gains. This longer horizon helps investors handle the relatively high volatility of individual stocks relative to other investments. Finally, familiarity with the different investment vehicles, through reading, discussions, and experience, will lend itself to comfort and eventually investment in those vehicles.

As discussed, there are several factors to weigh when creating and managing a retirement portfolio. Apart from the previously mentioned points, one factor to consider is the level of diversification in your portfolio. All else equal, we want to increase our diversification without materially sacrificing our returns. Given that the majority of IRA accounts are rooted in stocks and bonds, it makes sense for us to find an appropriate balance between these two asset classes. Stocks have historically performed better than bonds over long time horizons (10 years and longer). At the same time, stocks have shown more volatile returns than bonds. Given this information, we will be looking to start with a higher percentage of stocks than bonds, to account for their higher historical returns. As we age, we'll look to decrease the weight of stocks in our portfolio, while replacing that change with an increase in bonds. The closer you get to retirement age, the less time you have to make up any losses that you incur.

For those looking to reduce investment risk as they age automatically, target-date funds might be a good option. These funds start with a higher percentage of allocation towards stocks. As we age, the fund automatically shifts towards more fixed income products, which will naturally reduce both our risk and expected return. These funds are offered with different target retirement years. For example, when I started my first full-time job, I chose to allocate my 401(k) contributions to the 2060 Vanguard Target Date Fund. This fund is targeted towards those who are looking to retire between 2058 and 2062. The fund currently has an allocation of roughly 90% stocks and 10% bonds, with the weights shifting more towards bonds slowly as the years go on.

As mentioned, investors consider bonds to be safer than stocks as an investment. When you buy a bond, you only profit from the company paying off that bond, which happens before any equity holders can claim any profits from the company's operations. For a younger person who can stand some swings in their portfolio, I would recommend heavy weightings towards stocks, certainly above 75%. For the most risk-tolerant, I would say that 90% stocks and 10% bonds would be a healthy mix. These numbers are going to be skewed higher than they used to be, mostly due to people living longer today than they have in the past. The old rule-of-thumb for your target stock weight was previously found by taking 100 and subtracting your age. Under this rule, a 25-year-old would have 75% of their portfolio in stocks and the rest in bonds. Similarly, a 50-year-old person would have a portfolio consisting of half stocks and half bonds. This allocation would be considered extremely conservative by today's standards, as retirees will likely need to hold more stocks later in life than what was previously recommended. I've read that some people like to keep this as a good guideline, but just change the starting number from 100 to 120. Using this updated rule, a 50-year-old investor with around 15 years to retirement would keep approximately 70% of her portfolio in stocks, with 30% in bonds. This allocation provides a more appropriate mix of stocks and bonds for someone who will want to maximize their time in retirement. Fewer stocks and more bonds would, on average, forego gains for safety. Even as you draw from your portfolio in retirement, a small part of your portfolio would be in stocks under this rule. Having a portion of your funds in stocks results in further capital appreciation for the later years of your life.

Within 401(k)s specifically, it makes sense to hold a diversified portfolio of either mutual funds or ETFs. A strategy that includes a mix of companies both large and small can often help us achieve our retirement goals while reducing company-specific risks. Recently, I've been thinking about an asset allocation for a young investor that might be split into four equal parts. This idea is an offshoot of Dave Ramsey's 25/25/25/25 allocation. In this case, we can focus 75% on U.S. stocks of different sizes and the remainder on international stocks. I've detailed the allocation as follows:

- 25% large-cap stocks
- 25% mid-cap stocks
- 25% small-cap stocks
- 25% international stocks

Such an allocation will increase your exposure to companies of all sizes and geographic locations. This suggestion could be a good starting point for your 401(k) portfolio.

A convenient feature about IRAs is that you have more control over your individual investments. You can also better control the weight of those investments within your portfolio. If you are towards the more risk-averse side of the spectrum, you can tailor your portfolio to fit that requirement. You can opt to follow the handy guidelines I had mentioned, or you can scrap both of those and go your own way. Conversely, you don't have this option in a 401(k). Your employer will have a predetermined selection of funds to choose from, so once you select the general fund(s), you don't have any control over asset allocation. You'll want to keep the following thought in mind when you are determining your yearly retirement contributions. If you think you can manage your investments better than any of your 401(k) plans, then you should allocate more money to your IRA. If you like the idea of passive contributions where you don't have to do any legwork, then you should heavily consider increasing your 401(k) contributions.

Taking a further dive into our portfolio, we'll start to wonder about the nuances of the portfolio allocation we've chosen. It seems simple enough to determine a proposed mix of 70% stocks, 30% bonds or 50% stocks, 50% bonds. How do we go beyond that and choose which stocks and bonds to buy? To gain exposure to stocks or bonds, we can use either individual stocks/bonds or funds that invest in these securities. We can further separate funds into ETFs (exchange-traded funds) and mutual funds, which can either be actively managed or benchmarked to an index. Though we went over these terms when discussing investing, they still might sound foreign, so I will go over them quickly. A mutual fund is an entity through which money managers pool money from many investors and use the proceeds to purchase securities. An ETF is similar to a mutual fund, except these types of funds trade on exchanges (just like individual stocks and bonds do). Mutual funds tend to have investment minimums, such as $1,000 or $3,000, whereas ETFs do not have minimums but instead have a price per share, just like individual stocks.

Suppose you wanted to focus your portfolio on the financial services sector. To achieve the proper diversification across the industry, you could invest in several different companies in that industry directly. For example, you could log into your account and buy shares of Bank of America, Citigroup, Morgan Stanley, and Goldman Sachs, among others. Although you wouldn't achieve sector diversification, you would reduce your exposure to company-specific risks using this strategy. However, you could forego the time-consuming nature of this process by choosing to invest in a mutual fund or ETF that tracks an index of financial sector companies. For the financial sector, a good example is the Vanguard Financials ETF (VFH). Vanguard designed this ETF to track the MSCI US Investable Market Financials Index. It has a meager expense ratio of 0.10%. This figure means that if you were to hold the security for one year, you would pay a total of $10 for every $10,000 of the security that you own. Given that expense ratios used to be much higher, retail investors have certainly welcomed this broad-scale reduction of fees due to the advent of both Vanguard funds and ETFs. Also, since index funds are passively managed, they come with lower expense ratios than active mutual funds, which attempt to beat a benchmark or index.

The truth about actively managed mutual funds is that most fail to beat their benchmark, and most of the time, they charge higher fees than the comparable index fund. Higher fees result in performance below the baseline most of the time. Years of data show this to be true: a Standard & Poors report published at the end of 2016 showed that more than 90% of fund managers failed to achieve even benchmark performance. Only about 8% of large-cap managers, 5% of mid-cap managers, and 7% of small-cap managers succeeded in reaching or beating their respective benchmarks over a 15-year period. Hedge funds, another type of fund, have become famous for charging high fees such as the infamous 2/20 (2% of assets under management and 20% of all gains). Seeing renowned hedge fund managers such as Seth Klarman and Bill Ackman post market-beating gains year after year piques the interest of active investors everywhere. The issue with hedge funds is that the minimum investments are very high, generally over $1 million. These funds also have self-imposed caps on assets under management, as the more assets you have, the lower your maximum expected return on investment. These restrictions make investing in hedge funds impractical for most investors. Luckily, we can do very well in their absence.

For retirement planning, your best bet will be to stick with index funds and the occasional stock pick, especially early in your career. The reason I suggest stock-picking early on is that you have so much time to make up any potential losses from choices that don't work out. Any investor you ask will tell you that not all stock picks work out, even for the best like Warren Buffett. His investment in IBM was undoubtedly a disappointment, but that pick certainly does not define his career. However, it likely won't be in your best interest to fund your retirement solely using individual stock picks. On the following page, I've made a list of the four reasons why you should heavily consider using index funds to help you achieve your retirement goals:

- Immediate diversification.
- No company-related risk, so no need to worry about picking the wrong company.
- Historical returns are higher than 8% for the S&P 500 over the long run (40+ years). Note that these do not guarantee future performance, but it's good to know history nonetheless.
- Small expense ratios and a low price for diversification (.04% is $4 per $10,000 per year).

Let's go over each of these points in greater detail. Index funds give you immediate diversification of your funds with only a few button clicks. Choosing an index fund will save an immense amount of time for you, as you won't have to research stocks for hours on end when you could be pursuing other hobbies. You're diversifying your investment over whichever category you choose. There are many to choose from, so you won't have any issues finding what you need. You can diversify over asset class, sectors of the economy, value/growth characteristics, and dividend payout characteristics, among others.

In choosing to use index funds, you diversify company risk away. We can define company risk as the risk an investor takes when holding a stock of a single company. An example could be holding the stock of a beverage company, where declining sales and increasing costs could drive profits downward. Even as the rest of the market does well, your beverage company is disappointing investors, and you have nothing to offset that. In this situation, your company could lose substantial market value (50%) in a certain period, as investors become disillusioned. However, had you held an index fund that owns this company, over the same period, the loss would undoubtedly prove to be lesser in magnitude. This idea makes sense because the fund invests in many other companies. As such, the returns of the index are not dependent on any particular company. Instead, the performance is spread out over many companies. Diversification has several different levels, such as being diversified between asset classes, between sectors, and between other classifications of stocks such as value/growth. Choosing an S&P 500 index fund would get you broad diversification across the spectrum of industries, but not necessarily size (as the S&P 500 does not include small-cap companies). Similarly, an index fund that tracks a financial index would give you diversification across the financial companies themselves, but none across the other sectors of the economy.

Another reason to choose an index fund (specifically an S&P 500 fund) is that the stock market has excellent compounded returns over long periods. Research shows that from 1928 to 2014, the lowest-returning 40 year period yielded a gain of 8.9% per year, while the highest-returning period yielded 12.5%. To illustrate the power of this return over the period, let us consider an example using the worst 40-year performance stated. If you were to invest $6,000 at the end of every year for 40 years at an 8.9% return, your final balance after 40 years would be $1,973,741.38. If we reduce the contribution to $5,000, we still end up with $1,644,784.48. Here she is, our old friend *compound interest*. There is a reason that Albert Einstein said compound interest is the "eighth wonder of the world." It seems that the simplest way to earn more over the long term is to start earlier. On an average basis, returns increase with each passing year. Of course, profits are rarely linear, but we must consider the idea that over the long-term, average volatility decreases. Your returns, though potentially choppy in the short-term, will more than likely smooth out over 40 years of investing. Taking another look at the best and worst 40-year returns listed, we are comforted to know that past investors have been rewarded handsomely for taking a long view. Because of this, I would advise that you start as early as is feasible. As we've said before, there truly is no better time than the present to start investing (you'll see through life that this rule is applicable outside of personal finance as well).

   The final point I want to make concerning the benefits of index funds involves the cost structure. As previously mentioned, mutual funds and ETFs charge expense ratios instead of commissions. Index funds often have lower expense ratios than actively-managed mutual funds. The 'Vanguard 500 Admiral Shares' index fund boasts an expense ratio of 0.04%, which translates to an annual cost of $4 for every $10,000 under management. Actively-managed funds tend to run above 0.50% and sometimes creep up to 1%, depending on where you're looking. An example comparable to the Vanguard 500 Admiral Shares fund might be the John Hancock Fundamental Large Cap Core Fund, which has a total expense ratio of 0.78%. Thus, this fund costs almost 20 times more than does the Vanguard fund. This extra cost might not be a concern when you are comparing prices of $78 and $4, but what about when your portfolio grows? Perhaps you'd eventually be looking at costs of $7,800 and $400 because the value of your account is $1 million. This example attempts to highlight the advantage of index funds from a cost-cutting perspective. If you are further interested in the impact of fees on portfolio returns, NerdWallet published a fantastic article on this topic (which can be found in the References section at the back of this book).

Given that I was so eager to illuminate the benefits of using index funds for retirement, I think it is only fair to examine some of the drawbacks of these investment vehicles. One disadvantage is the lack of flexibility. When the index in question is performing poorly, an index fund manager doesn't have many options to limit the losses. They are constrained to their goal of matching the returns of the index, even if those returns are negative. Active mutual funds thrive within this dynamic. Managers will be able to react to market movements and adjust the holdings and weights based on what they see. They aren't bound to the index returns, weights, or holdings. If you value this advantage, active funds are certainly something to consider.

Another disadvantage of index funds is that they cannot outpace the market or participate in severe mispricing opportunities. Whereas an active manager might be able to locate a mispricing and take advantage of it, an index fund manager isn't able to deviate materially from the weights of the index. Creativity in stock-picking is severely limited here. If that point is a concern for you, active funds could have a place in your portfolio.

When saving for retirement, we have to remember that it is a very long game. Depending on your planning skills and dedication to your goals, this could turn out to be either positive or negative. If you use that time for good, you will set yourself up to benefit from compounded growth over a significant number of years. However, if you fail to start investing early because you believe you can catch up when you're older, you might be setting yourself up for a tough road ahead. One of the most important things to remember about long-term investing is that having more time is always preferable to having less time. To illustrate the difference between starting early and catching up later, imagine you invest $1,000 into an account that earned 7% a year, and you contribute annually for 40 years. At the end of 40 years, you would have about $199,000. In a different scenario, you choose to invest $2,000 a year for 30 years at the same rate. You would end up with $188,000, about $11,000 less than you would have had you chosen the first plan. Even though we doubled the yearly contribution amount, we were still not able to overcome the damage due to missed time. This example illustrates the power of starting your investment timeline as early as possible.

 Another thing to note is that you can be successful as an investor and saver without having a complicated strategy that involves derivatives, options, and lots of trading. Keeping the investing process simple will help streamline your decisions so you can focus on other things in your life that are enjoyable. As much as I enjoy writing this, I understand that there are other things to do and other hobbies to enjoy. In the spirit of this work, we should aim to devise a strategy that is as simple as possible. Jack Bogle, the pioneer who founded Vanguard in 1975, was the most vocal proponent of this idea. In creating the first index fund, he helped millions of investors reach their goals by giving them a simple way to take advantage of diversification and compounded growth. If you are concerned that stock-picking will take up too much of your time, or if you don't want to be bothered at all, consider an index fund. It certainly doesn't have to be Vanguard, although I can say from experience that they have a great platform. Schwab, Fidelity, and T. Rowe Price all offer index funds that will track the S&P 500, among other indices. These funds might have slightly different weights assigned to particular holdings within the fund. Given this, it would be prudent to read the prospectus' and fact sheets of the funds you are considering before you make your investment decision.

 One of the most important things to realize about retirement investing is that it's okay to start with a small sum of funds. With apps like Stash and Robinhood making it easy to buy fractional shares and allowing you to auto-buy every period, consistent investing has never been easier. That's important because being able to consistently invest in either a basket of securities or a single security takes so much stress out of investing. Choosing when to buy and when to sell has always been difficult. Even the best investors have difficulty with the latter half of the buy/sell sequence.

With consistent investing, we buy more shares when prices are lower and fewer shares when prices are higher. One well-known version of this is dollar-cost averaging (DCA), which we talked about in the Investing chapter. This term refers to the act of investing a uniform amount of money at regular intervals. This type of strategy mitigates the emotional attachment to your investments, which is something that many investors have trouble taming. It's hard to invest in a stock that is on a downtrend continually. I can understand the frustration that comes with owning (and adding to) a position that's taken a wrong turn. However, if you think about it, you can still make money in a downturn because you'll be buying some shares at lower prices, and over time accumulate more shares. If you invest a lump sum intending to never add to the position, you are very much susceptible to a potential decrease in the stock price. You have no way to profit from a decrease if you don't buy-in again at a lower price. Burton Malkiel describes this principle with great eloquence in his seminal work, "A Random Walk Down Wall Street." I very much recommend the book, even though I don't believe markets are efficient enough to warrant the absence of individual stocks within a portfolio. The piece on dollar-cost averaging is enlightening and goes into great detail on how investors who start early can succeed using this simple strategy. In addition to removing emotions from investing, DCA builds discipline by sticking to a plan, in good times and in bad. It's a test of emotional fortitude. However, DCA investors might be more comforted by their strategy, as they won't have to worry as much about a short or medium-term decline in value. They know that during those downtimes, they will be buying shares, just as they had the previous period. If you are concerned about the value of your investment declining in the short term after your purchase, DCA could prove to be a fruitful option for you. DCA can also work for you if you don't happen to have money available right from the start.

Invariably, one must examine the pitfalls of using DCA to get the most accurate picture of the strategy. One potential pitfall is that you might achieve lower returns than you would have had you invested all the money upfront. This idea is especially true if the price continually increases over some time, with little to no decreases below the initial investment price. Studies have shown this idea to be true. Vanguard recently published a study highlighting that lump-sum investing returns are higher than DCA returns about two-thirds of the time. They also noted that "risk-averse investors may be less concerned about averages than they are about worst-case scenarios, as well as the potential feelings of regret that would occur if a lump-sum investment were made immediately prior to a market decline." However, since it might not be possible to invest that lump sum at the beginning of the investing period, this might not make much of a practical difference. Another downside to DCA is that it isn't designed with individual stocks in mind. When you DCA into a stock, you are still exposed to company risk. You can't eradicate this risk without proper diversification.

Additionally, DCA doesn't take the inevitability of new company developments into account. If something happens to a firm that changes your outlook on the company, it might force you to reconsider your investment strategy. Since DCA technically requires consistency in both frequency and magnitude of investments, it's not the nimblest strategy in that regard. In my mind, DCA is best suited for ETFs and mutual funds, where you're holding a basket of investments as opposed to a single company-specific investment. If you wish to use DCA as part of your investing strategy, I recommend setting up automatic fund transfers from your bank account. This way, the investment would become a more passive choice. This tweak could prove fruitful during periods of negative stock returns when it becomes emotionally tougher to continue putting money in the markets.

For both retirement and taxable accounts, there are companies such as Wealthfront and Betterment that will automatically diversify your portfolio among different asset classes. I personally use Wealthfront and find it to be a great way to transform my portfolio from being all-equities to also including asset classes such as real estate, natural resources, and municipal bonds. Algorithms entirely drive this process, which attempts to allocate your funds according to your risk tolerance by investing in related ETFs and other exchange-traded securities. Here's how it works:

- Fill out a survey related to your investing experience, as well as your willingness and ability to take risks. The app assigns you a risk tolerance score, which can change at any time if you wish to take the survey at a later point (they understand that things change!).
- Choose between a taxable brokerage account, an IRA, or a Roth IRA.
- Deposit an initial investment, which the app will then allocate to different asset classes (the choice of these will depend on the risk tolerance score you received in Step 1).
- Going forward, you can select your investment frequency and amount. If you'd prefer to decide that when the time comes, you can default to the manual option as well.

One feature embedded into both Wealthfront and Betterment that we haven't emphasized is tax-loss harvesting. When deemed appropriate, these apps will simultaneously sell a security and buy a very similar security to lock in taxable losses. These apps can do this because many ETFs will track the same index or use the same (or similar) strategy. Automatic tax-loss harvesting will allow you to claim more losses on your tax returns while keeping the investments in-line with your allocations and risk tolerance. I implore you to at least research these options (and other roboadvisors) that are available[3].

You might be noticing a few common themes that have permeated throughout most chapters of this text. One is likely the idea that consistency and diligence are crucial to success within many of the facets of personal finance we've discussed.

---

[3] My only experience has been with Wealthfront and I am not insinuating that I fully understand the intricacies of Betterment or other roboadvising services currently being offered.

Another is that we can use technology to automate many of the tasks we previously accomplished manually. For example, instead of sending monthly checks to mutual fund companies via mail, we can set up monthly recurring deposits on our phones. A final theme, especially regarding investing, might be that starting early can help give you the best chance for success.

Before we conclude this chapter, we should touch on two very important topics within the context of retirement planning: Social Security and our goals by age. The former is perhaps the most popular government assistance program in the world, while the latter involves a system of benchmarks that are helpful to you as a retirement saver. Possessing knowledge of these two key areas will help you achieve your retirement goals.

As mentioned, almost all Americans know of the Social Security system. It has been the preeminent retirement savings program since its inception in 1935 when it was introduced to Congress by President Franklin D. Roosevelt. At the time, America was still reeling from the Great Depression, and our leaders were looking for ways to prevent a similar situation from happening again. With this goal in mind, FDR had an idea for a social program designed to support workers 65 years and older with a continued income for the rest of their lives. This program has since expanded from its humble beginnings in 1935 to a program that doled out $615 billion in 2008. It is an often-politicized issue that makes its way into presidential debates, campaign ads, and newspaper columns with great frequency. We aim to understand both how the program works and how we can account for Social Security within our retirement plan.

First, let's briefly explore the basics of how Social Security (SS) works. The Social Security Administration (SSA), which is the government agency currently presiding over the program, explains it this way: When you work, you pay taxes into the SS system. The government then uses those funds to pay benefits to:

- "People who have already retired.
- People who are disabled.
- Survivors of workers who have died.
- Dependents of beneficiaries."

Similar to how banks operate, the SSA does not place funds into a personal vault with your name on it. The SSA transfers the money you pay to those who receive benefits today. In a sense, we are transferring funds from the young to the elderly. 85% of every Social Security tax dollar goes into a trust that pays current retirees and their families. In comparison, 15% goes towards paying people with disabilities and their families. The government intended this program to be a supplement to other sources of retirement income. Unfortunately, too many Americans have had issues because there is significant reliance on SS to carry us through retirement with no other sources of income. The preceding conversation about 401(k)s and IRAs serves to instill the idea that we can control our destiny outside of what Social Security can provide. While we can consider Social Security to be a successful government program, it cannot supply all that we need to retire. This unfortunate truth is why 401(k)s and IRAs have been part of the conversation for many years and will continue to be relevant in the future.

It's important to understand that Social Security will only replace a fraction of your earnings upon retirement. Higher earnings during your career years will translate to increased benefits once you start to collect SS. If you wait until your full retirement age, you will receive your full retirement benefits. Continuing this idea, if you choose to delay receiving these benefits until after your full retirement age, your future monthly benefit increases by a certain percentage. This increase in future benefits will increase until you start claiming benefits or when you reach age 70, whichever comes first. You can also take benefits as early as age 62. Still, in the same vein as before, your benefits will decrease if you start to claim SS earlier than your full retirement age.

If you haven't yet reached the age of 62, Social Security might appear to be a distant concept. Depending on your current age, you might not be able to claim SS for some time. However, it's always great to set a solid foundation upon which you can build a fortress of knowledge. One relatable scenario is that your parents might need advice on when to take Social Security either now or in the future. On this, there seem to be several schools of thought.

A standard recommendation is to delay benefits for as long as possible. This action will maximize your future monthly income and is an excellent option for those of you who have built up enough savings to take you through those interim years comfortably. Another idea is to take the benefits at 62 and continually invest the funds in stocks, bonds, or other investments. With this strategy, we are taking advantage of receiving the funds eight years earlier than we would if we claimed full benefits at age 70. Any rational investor should think that the time value of money would work in our favor. Nevertheless, the success of this strategy will depend on the investments made over the period, which should directly correlate with the risks taken during portfolio allocation.

In my view, if you are able to wait at least several years after age 62 and you aren't looking to invest the SS proceeds, there isn't much reason for you to claim benefits early. Of course, there will be folks reading this who will depend more on the benefits provided by SS. If you fit this description, I would say that you've earned the benefits offered to you by SS. You should take them at your full discretion. As a simple rule-of-thumb, if you can try to wait as long as possible to claim your benefits, your patience will be rewarded into perpetuity. As a bonus, this reward won't require any extra effort on your part.

For more than 80 years, Social Security has helped millions of Americans through retirement by creating a system of forced savings. It continues to be an essential part of the retirement picture, so I'm glad we covered it here, and I'm hoping you took something from the discussion. Given that you'll spend most of your adult life paying into the system, it is in your best interest to understand how the system works and how you can plan to make the best use of it.

A final point regarding retirement planning involves goal-setting. As with other facets of personal finance, goal-setting is an integral part of retirement planning. In this arena, benchmarks are most commonly set by age, though you can tweak this any which way to fit your style. I personally like Fidelity's parameters, which are set out as follows: "Aim to save at least 1x your salary by 30, 3x by 40, 6x by 50, 8x by 60, and 10x by 67." If you're younger than 30, your first objective would be to save the amount of your pre-tax salary.

Similarly, if you're between 30 and 40 years of age, your next benchmark will be saving three times your income by age 40. If you work in an industry where your income is variable, you might need to assume a baseline figure for now. You can probably take the average of your previous three years of income as a decent proxy. These benchmarks won't work as well if you expect to earn above-average raises later in your career. Let's assume you start your career earning $50,000 per year at age 22. You earn designations and put in the work to make a salary of $100,000 at age 30. By these metrics, you should have $100,000 saved by age 30. This rule fails to take into account the 9% average growth in salary you achieved in the eight years between age 22 and age 30. If you find yourself unable to meet these benchmarks yet, please don't be discouraged. In these situations, your best course of action is to focus on the present and future. Those earlier in their careers might be best served by contributing more to a growth-oriented portfolio. At the same time, those later in life might contemplate increasing savings, reducing expenses, and working longer than previously anticipated. As with any heuristics, these rules-of-thumb are not perfect but do represent worthwhile objectives to keep you on track for the future. If you're able to hit these, you will be in great shape, especially when considering the added benefits received from Social Security once you start to claim them.

Let's recap what we learned about retirement planning:

- We can split retirement investing accounts into two overarching categories: 401(k)s, which are sponsored by employers, and IRAs, which are opened by individuals such as yourself. Within both of these, there are two options: Traditional, which grants a tax deferral now in exchange for taxation upon withdrawal, and Roth, which does not grant any tax deferral today but frees you from any obligation going forward (so long as you follow all relevant

guidelines).
- We dove further into index funds and how they can give us instant diversification at a low cost.
- Continuing the theme of the previous paragraph, we learned that starting early can lead to improved results. We looked at two contribution scenarios and noticed that contributing less per month for a more extended period can yield better results than contributing more for a short period.
- Bouncing off the previous point, we saw that small contributions can add up and compound over time. Please don't think that a small contribution amount today won't make a dent over time. We all need to start somewhere, and getting started on this journey can be one of the best decisions of your life.
- You can be as involved as you'd like. With the automation of deposits, portfolios, and transactions, there's no longer any pressure to take an active role in sending checks or selecting investments. Of course, if you're interested in taking a more active part in the process, you are free to do that as well.
- Social Security is an integral part of the American financial fabric, and using it to our advantage is critical. Delaying your realization of benefits can be a good option if you can afford to do so. You could also take the benefits earlier and invest the funds.
- Setting goals and following appropriate benchmarks can help keep us on the path to success. We discussed rules-of-thumb provided by Fidelity and how they are not precise deadlines, but rather heuristics used to guide our financial decisions.

Conclusion

Personal finance is a subject that has gripped me since I was old enough to understand the importance it has in our lives. Ever since I started diving into markets and how money works, I've become fascinated with wealth creation and preservation. I love personal finance because I believe it's something that I can optimize. I often spend a reasonable amount of time thinking about optimization of account choice, investments, risks, career moves, and other factors that play into wealth creation. I'm excited to share my thoughts on personal finance within this book. Just as a guitar player learns more about music every day, I always challenge myself and find new things to discover within personal finance. Perhaps this project will be the springboard that introduces another part of myself to the world, a piece that opens my creative mind to new possibilities and endeavors.

Wealth creation is something that takes time. As the famous saying goes, Rome was not built in one day. In a similar vein, it would be foolish for us to believe that our financial position will materially improve in a short period. We can say the same for our physical health, mental health, and many other areas of our lives.

However, this does not mean that our decisions are fruitless. The choices we make today will affect our future state more so than our present state. The decision to create a budget won't turn your life around in one day. Still, the diligence and consistency that might follow have a good chance of changing the long-term trend for the better. Further, saving $200 this month might not make a difference right now, but you will notice that these choices will alter the course of your future.

I hope that we eventually teach personal finance as mandatory material in all high schools within the United States. Unfortunately, we seem to be far behind in this endeavor. According to a study by Next Gen Personal Finance, "just one in six high-schoolers in the U.S. are required to take at least one stand-alone personal-finance semester for graduation." Using this figure as an approximation, we can reasonably estimate that less than 20% of high school students end up taking a personal finance course. Some colleges (such as Stony Brook University, my alma mater) offer financial literacy seminars. Still, attendance at these gatherings could be better. Through conversations with people and reading news articles, it seems that many people are learning about personal finance through their use of phone apps. Examples of these include Stash, Robinhood, Wealthfront, and Betterment. The future of learning in this arena seems to be correlated with the popularity of these apps. In using them, you not only invest and save money but also learn why you are taking these actions and how these actions can help build your foundation over time.

    In writing this book, I attempted to teach the values that brought me to where I am today. I also found it worthwhile to include information regarding relevant accounts, plans, and options where necessary. I hope that this book helped you organize your financial life, and I hope it taught you a few things about yourself as well. If there's one thing that I learned from reading books, it's the following. Whether you're reading a book, watching a television show or movie, or examining a painting: if you can take one thing from that work with you going forward, that makes the work well worth your time. In my experience, no book I've read has been perfect from cover to cover, nor can I remember every detail from any given text. However, I can say that the books I put on the top of my list are those that taught me something, whether it was about myself, the world around me, or both. I hope that this is your experience here. Thank you for reading. Please consider leaving a review to help inform other readers about this book.

Acknowledgements

Writing this book was not a solo journey. Without the help of trusted family and friends, I wouldn't have been able to complete this work. Let me tell you the story of this book.

In February of 2019, I worked in my old office located at 250 Park Avenue. As I typed away at my computer, an idea popped in my head. I have a lot of useful knowledge related to personal finance. Is there any way I can share this knowledge with others? Soon after, I started to write my first draft. However, when the CFA Level I exam came along, I knew I needed to start studying. My development as a professional is very important to me, so I made sure to dedicate my time to studying for this crucial exam. I put my unfinished draft on the back burner for the time being.

In March of 2020, the COVID-19 pandemic hit the United States like a freight train. As of mid-March, I was working from home. With a lot more time on my hands, I wanted to make use of this unique time in history. After consulting with my girlfriend Rebecca, I decided to pursue completion of this book. I had only written about 10,000 words in this unfinished first draft, so I knew there was a lot of work left to be done. Over the next few months, I was able to complete and refine the text several times. The end result is the book you are reading right now.

I would first like to thank my wonderful girlfriend Rebecca, who was an immense help to me throughout the process. From the moment I completed my first draft, she was constantly helping me edit the text, create draft covers, and tighten up all loose ends. She's an absolute whiz when it comes to marketing, so I'm very grateful that she was willing to share her wisdom with me as I went through this process. Thank you for believing in me and supporting me through everything.

Of course, I would be nowhere without my family. Mom, Dad, and Michelle, thank you so much for believing in me and for always being there for me if I had any questions. The education, guidance, and wisdom I've obtained throughout my

24 years has been a testament to the strong, principled family that raised me. Thank you so much for supporting me and being confident in my abilities.

I also want to say thank you to Tommy Corrigan for the wonderful cover art. The cover looks fantastic and is not certainly something I could create on my own. I suppose everyone has their strong suits. Thank you for sharing yours! I hope to repay the favor someday soon.

Lastly, I would like to thank my friends. A few choice people have been in my life since elementary school, and I wouldn't be the person I am today without them. Zack, Chris, and Tyler, thank you all for being the best of friends. I can always count on you to support and be there for me if I ever need you. Our frequent encounters help to solidify our relationship, and we always enjoy each other's company.

Again, thank you to everyone who has helped me throughout this process. I appreciate each and every one of you. I hope to repay the favor in the future.

References

Introduction

1. Stock Investing for Dummies
   a. https://www.amazon.com/Stock-Investing-Dummies-Paul-Mladjenovic-dp-1119660769/dp/1119660769/ref=dp_ob_title_bk
      i. This book gives a great foundation to those looking to start investing.
2. Federal Reserve Board Report on Economic Well-Being of U.S. Households
   a. https://www.federalreserve.gov/newsevents/pressreleases/other20190523b.htm
      i. Provides background on financial standing of Americans.
      ii. Surveys conducted by the Federal Reserve give great insight into economic conditions.
3. IMF List of GDP per capita for all countries
   a. shorturl.at/acdvM
      i. Same idea as the Federal Reserve's surveys but on an international level
4. Pew Research Article Regarding U.S. Real Wage Stagnation
   a. https://www.pewresearch.org/fact-tank/2018/08/07/for-most-us-workers-real-wages-have-barely-budged-for-decades/
      i. Provides background on many economic and social issues.
      ii. Pew Research has a reputation for non-partisan research.

Chapter 1: The Power of the Mind

1. How 5 of America's Old Money Families Lost it All
   a. https://moneywise.com/a/how-5-of-americas-richest-families-lost-it-all
      i. Gives detail on how some of the largest American fortunes have been squandered.

Chapter 2: Budgeting

1. No links were attached within this chapter.

Chapter 3: Investing

1. Exchange Traded Fund: What is an ETF?
   a. https://www.investopedia.com/terms/e/etf.asp
      i. Explains what an ETF is and what its structure means for investors.

Chapter 4: Student Loans

1. A Look at the Shocking Student Loan Debt Statistics for 2020
   a. https://studentloanhero.com/student-loan-debt-statistics/
      i. Article explaining the state of student loan debt in the U.S. as of Jan. 15, 2020.
2. Federal Versus Private Loans
   a. https://studentaid.gov/understand-aid/types/loans/federal-vs-private
      i. Government webpage showcasing the differences between Federal Student Loans, Federal Parent Loans, and Private Student Loans.
3. Subsidized and Unsubsidized Loans
   a. https://studentaid.gov/understand-

aid/types/loans/subsidized-unsubsidized
- i. Government webpage showcasing the differences between Direct Subsidized Loans and Direct Unsubsidized Loans.
4. Federal Interest Rates and Fees
   a. https://studentaid.gov/understand-aid/types/loans/interest-rates
      i. Government webpage describing the interest rates and fees charged on Federal Student Loans.
5. Bankrate Loan Calculator
   a. https://www.bankrate.com/calculators/mortgages/loan-calculator.aspx
      i. Calculator that determines the monthly payments on a loan based on given inputs.
6. Debt Snowball Versus Debt Avalanche
   a. https://www.forbes.com/sites/robertberger/2017/07/20/debt-snowball-versus-debt-avalanche-what-the-academic-research-shows/#6ed41fb01454
      i. Article describing the psychological research conducted into the snowball and avalanche methods.

Chapter 5: Credit Card, Auto Loan, and Mortgage Debts

1. How Do Car Loans Work?
   a. https://www.policygenius.com/loans/how-do-car-loans-work/
      i. A great article which explains how car loans fit into the car-buying picture.
2. 10 Steps to Buying a Home
   a. https://www.discover.com/home-loans/articles/10-steps-to-buying-a-home/
      i. Article from Discover that gives 10 steps on how to purchase a home.
3. 28/36 Rule

a. https://www.investopedia.com/terms/t/twenty-eight-thirty-six-rule.asp
    i. Article from Investopedia detailing the 28/36 rule of home-buying.
4. Debt-to-Income Ratio Calculator
   a. https://www.wellsfargo.com/goals-credit/debt-to-income-calculator/
      i. Tool that calculates a person's DTI, given the relevant debt and income levels.

Chapter 6: Wedding and Marriage Planning

1. How Much Does the Average Wedding Cost?
   a. https://www.nerdwallet.com/article/finance/how-much-does-average-wedding-cost
      i. Article that details the various costs of a typical wedding.
2. Why More Millennials are Signing Prenups
   a. https://www.businessinsider.com/why-sign-a-prenup-marriage-divorce-2018-9
      i. Article that details why more millennials are starting to sign prenups.
3. Should Couples Have Joint or Separate Bank Accounts?
   a. https://www.thebalance.com/should-you-have-joint-or-separate-bank-accounts-1289664
      i. Evaluate the pros and cons of merging bank accounts with your spouse.
4. The Two Most Important Quotes in Business
   a. https://www.growthink.com/content/two-most-important-quotes-business
      i. Article containing a famous quote: "If you can't measure it, you can't improve it." I want to note here that I found some sources which stated that this quote is misattributed to management thinker Peter Drucker, but the phrase itself serves a purpose regardless of its orator.

Chapter 7: Planning College for Your Children

1. Explore Pros, Cons of Using Coverdell Accounts for College Savings
   a. https://www.usnews.com/education/best-colleges/paying-for-college/articles/2015/04/29/explore-pros-cons-of-using-coverdell-accounts-for-college-savings
      i. Article explaining the benefits and drawbacks of Coverdell Accounts.
2. College Cost Projector
   a. https://vanguard.wealthmsi.com/collcost.php
      i. Tool that calculates future cost of college based on given inputs.
      ii. This page also shows that the average increase in college costs has reached 5% in recent years.
3. How Much Should You Really Save for your Child's College?
   a. https://www.hermoney.com/borrow/student-loans/how-much-to-save-for-your-childs-college/
      i. Article detailing the goal of paying for one-third of the cost of college per child.
4. What if You Only Invested at Market Peaks?
   a. https://awealthofcommonsense.com/2014/02/worlds-worst-market-timer/
      i. Tells the story of Bob, an example person who only invests at the worst possible times, yet still does well for himself.
5. Name the Top 7 Benefits of 529 Plans
   a. https://www.savingforcollege.com/intro-to-529s/name-the-top-7-benefits-of-529-plans
      i. Provides a list of the top 7 benefits of using 529 plans to save for your child's college.

Chapter 8: Planning For Retirement

1. This is How Many Fund Managers Actually Beat Index Funds
    a. https://www.marketwatch.com/story/why-way-fewer-actively-managed-funds-beat-the-sp-than-we-thought-2017-04-24
        i. Article with statistics about the number of fund managers that beat their benchmark.
2. Understanding Performance: The S&P 500 Index
    a. https://www.marketwatch.com/story/understanding-performance-the-sp-500-in-2015-02-18
        i. Article with statistics about historical S&P 500 performance.
3. How a 1% Fee Could Cost Millennials $590,000 in Retirement Savings
    a. https://www.nerdwallet.com/blog/investing/millennial-retirement-fees-one-percent-half-million-savings-impact/
        i. Article detailing how reducing investment fees can have an outsized impact on retirement savings outcomes.
4. Dollar-Cost Average Just Means Taking Risk Later
    a. https://static.twentyoverten.com/5980d16bbfb1c93238ad9c24/rJpQmY8o7/Dollar-Cost-Averaging-Just-Means-Taking-Risk-Later-Vanguard.pdf
        i. Note by Vanguard Research on DCA vs. Lump-Sum Investing (LSI).
5. History of Social Security
    a. https://www.ssa.gov/history/briefhistory3.html#:~:text=The%20Social%20Security%20Act%20was,a%20continuing%20income%20after%20retirement.
        i. Extremely detailed webpage that discusses the founding of Social Security in the U.S.

6. Understanding the Benefits of Social Security
    a. https://www.ssa.gov/pubs/EN-05-10024.pdf
        i. Document created by the SSA that describes how Social Security operates.
7. How Much Do I Need to Retire?
    a. https://www.fidelity.com/viewpoints/retirement/how-much-do-i-need-to-retire#:~:text=Fidelity's%20rule%20of%20thumb%3A%20Aim,are%20ways%20to%20catch%20up.
        i. Useful information from Fidelity on retirement rules-of-thumb and other retirement considerations.
8. Why Do So Many U.S. Schools Ignore Personal-Finance Education?
    a. https://www.marketwatch.com/story/want-to-develop-financially-capable-americans-teachers-may-be-even-more-important-than-laws-2019-09-20
        i. Article detailing why so few high school students are educated on personal finance matters, and how we could try to change this dilemma.

Index

"

"50/30/20" rule, 13

2

28/36 Rule, 69, 120

4

401(k), 87, 92, 93, 94, 95, 97, 99

5

529 plans, 79, 80, 86, 87, 88, 89, 90, 122

A

A Random Walk Down Wall Street, 30, 106
APR, 53, 61
assets, 5, 19, 23, 31, 32, 34, 49, 51, 54, 57, 75, 76, 101
avalanche method, 18, 19, 44, 46

B

Betterment, 107, 108, 115
bond, 19, 68, 71, 76, 81, 97
brokerage account, 88, 89, 108
buffer, 13, 14, 16, 17, 19, 21, 29, 31, 32, 69, 71

C

capital, 5, 17, 22, 23, 25, 26, 29, 31, 32, 40, 82, 84, 89, 98
ChangEd, 50
circle of competence, 24, 28
Common stocks, 23
compound interest, 3, 19, 20, 32, 34, 40, 90, 103
credit cards, 19, 51, 52, 53, 54, 55, 56, 59, 60, 64, 70, 71

D

DCA, 30, 31, 106, 107, 123
debit card, 55, 56, 58
Direct Consolidation Loans, 43
Direct Plus Loans, 42
Direct Subsidized Loans, 37, 38, 39, 41, 120
Direct Unsubsidized Loans, 38, 41, 42, 120
diversification, 96, 97, 100, 101, 102, 105, 107, 113
Dollar Cost Averaging, 30
down payment, 61

E

earnings per share, 25, 26
Efficient Market Hypothesis, 28
emergency fund, 4, 16, 17, 19, 46
ETF, 33, 100, 119
Excel, 8, 11, 16

F

Federal student loans, 37

finance, 1, 18, 73, 114
financial literacy, 115

G

goals by age, 109

I

index funds, 33, 84, 93, 100, 101, 102, 103, 104, 105, 113
interest rates, 20, 37, 38, 41, 43, 46, 52, 54, 70, 120

L

liabilities, 8, 17, 40, 52, 57, 60, 75, 76

M

microsaving, 44, 49, 50
Microsoft, 1, 8, 24
mindset, 4, 19, 37, 83
mortgages, 19, 51, 52, 54, 58, 60, 65, 69, 70, 71
Mutual Funds, 33

N

needs, 5, 12, 13, 14, 17, 21, 29, 34, 39, 47, 70, 94, 95

P

P/E Multiple, 26
pen-and-paper budget, 11

personal finance, 1, 2, 4, 5, 6, 16, 18, 34, 47, 52, 64, 73, 103, 108, 111, 114, 116, 124
private student loans, 37, 42, 43, 44
Projected Balance, 9

R

required minimum distributions, 93
risk tolerance, 27, 69, 96, 108

S

S&P 500, 22, 23, 32, 33, 101, 102, 105, 123
shares, 1, 23, 25, 28, 30, 33, 100, 105, 106
snowball method, 18, 19, 44
Social Security, 109, 110, 111, 112, 113, 123, 124

T

The Intelligent Investor, 28
time horizon, 20, 27, 32, 97

V

Vanguard, 68, 81, 83, 95, 97, 100, 103, 105, 107, 123

W

wants, 6, 9, 12, 13, 17
Wealthfront, 107, 108, 115

Z

Zero-Based Budgeting, 11, 21

www.ingramcontent.com/pod-product-compliance
Lightning Source LLC
Chambersburg PA
CBHW020433220526
45464CB00002B/691